Explore
the Right Approach to Write

Develop Effective Communication Skills

Daisy London

A.D.R.(London) Limited England

ADR's Publishing Motto

'A person who searches for knowledge is a student'

Copyright © A.D.R.(London)Limited 2005

British Library Cataloguing in Publication Data

A catalogue record for this book is available from the British Library

ISBN 190 1197 034

First published by A.D.R. in UK 2005

Warning and Disclaimer

Direct Order

In case of difficulty, you can obtain a copy from the publisher:

A.D.R. (London) Limited
24 St. Alban Road
Bridlington
YO16 7SS
England

Tel: 01262 605538/400323
Fax: 01262 400323
E-mail: sales@ adrlondon.ltd.uk
Web Site: www.adrlondon.ltd.uk

Printed in Great Britain

Contents

Part 2 Punctuation

Contents V

Part 3 Troublesome Words and Phrases

Part 4 Get Down to Communicate

Introduction

A particular way of written communication that enables you to create an effective link between yourself and the reader is the right approach to write. This simple idea does not imply that you, the writer, will always succeed in doing something by virtue of this writing approach. As in any real life situation, there are often some crucial issues that hinder the success you wish to make through the right approach to write. In essence, the right approach to write will enable you:

- to communicate with individuals, and all kinds of small and large organisations with self-confidence and self-reliance, and thus

- to state and present the content of your communication clearly towards the achievement of your objectives.

The right approach to write is primarily concerned with the day-to-day writing such as social letters, business correspondence, curriculum vitae(CV), job application, and similar writing activities. It is not intended for speech writers, journalists and novelists. Indeed, it is for you who has picked it up from a shelf and is enthusiastic about writing as a student, teacher, chemist, engineer, or someone who takes writing seriously.

You may be a native speaker or a learner of Standard English (also standard English). Standard English is socially accepted as the most correct form of the English language. It is the medium of communication used by text book writers, broadcasting authorities, newspapers, educational organisations, government agencies, etc. in Britain.

The art of writing is not a mystery. It is not shrouded in secrecy. It can be learnt and your writing skills can be developed to the highest level of personal accomplishment through practice over a period of time. Indeed, some people take longer to master the art of writing. Do not despair! You will get there. How?

The simple requirement is that you must learn and practise the fundamentals of the right approach to write. These fundamentals are:

words - the building blocks of both speech and writing. Words make up the language. No one expects you to know about one million words of the English language, which constitutes the English language **vocabulary**. For the right approach to write, a good vocabulary is an essential ingredient.

A sound knowledge of the English language vocabulary by itself does not enable anyone to communicate effectively without the knowledge and skill of using correct **grammar**. Grammar is about words of a language and how to combine them together into meaningful phrases, clauses and sentences.

The correct application of **rules of grammar** creates a grammatical structure that is meaningful, which the recipient of your letter can understand. Indeed, the success of your communication is not wholly based on the correct use of both vocabulary and grammar alone. It is **the content** of your communication that you want to convey to the recipient. If it does not come up to the expectation of the recipient, your communication will not create the right or desirable result. This is what I mean in the opening paragraph, "... real life situation... hinder the success..."

You are not a journalist who wants to create some sensation for the local or national populace. You are someone who wants to send a clear message to the recipient. This requires **a distinct method** of organising, writing and presenting the communication to the recipient/correspondent. The essential prerequisite is that you should be able to organise your thoughts about the matter being dealt with, and free your mind from other things. The freedom from confusion about the content of the communication will make it easy for you to plan, prepare, write and revise your communication.

The means of communication is the language. There are a number of styles of using the language, such as simple, complex, colourful, prose style, and so on. We are concerned here, mostly, with **the simple style** of using English. Indeed, if it is a communication between two experts then the use of technical words cannot be avoided, and the style of writing can become complex. Thus, it is also important to bear in mind at all times who your readers are. Your style of writing for effective communication should be simple, which calls for short phrases, clauses and sentences. It means you have to refrain from using complicated words, colourful language, jargon, etc.

Of course, you must know or imagine who is going to be the reader of your communication. If you are an engineer and dealing with the business communication, your style of writing will involve technical terms. Your written communication to another engineer will not sound complicated or full of jargon(technical terms). On the other hand, as an engineer, if you have to write to a layperson, then you must simplify your technical terms, so that you can achieve your aim of writing in a friendly manner. Therefore, the writing style is no less important than any other requirements described above. Finally, you are not a machine, but a human being. This gives you an opportunity of examining, with a view to learning, other people's writing, so that you can continue improving your own writing. Lifelong learning is the main theme nationally in Britain at the beginning of the 21st century! It makes all of us learners, and you are not alone. In this book , you will find:

Part 1 – it is concerned with the explanation of the essential principles (rules) of Standard English grammar. Numerous examples are included to help the reader to explore the application of the basic rules in order to construct phrases, clauses and sentences.

Part 2 – it explains and exemplifies the application of punctuation marks and the corresponding rules of using them correctly.

Part 3 – it has many troublesome words and phrases which often confuse some writers. These are listed and discussed in an A-Z order.

Part 4 – it describes the main requirements for developing written communication for social, business and official purposes. It gives scores of examples of written communication, so that the reader can see these as model writing.

Glossary - the glossary contains an alphabetical list of the definition of terms used in this book. It is of great help for a quick reference.

Index – the book finishes with an index.

Your learning needs may not be the same as those of many equally enthusiastic readers. It is, therefore, recognized that all readers will not read this book from the beginning to the end consecutively. Indeed, you can use it for reference purposes, as it contains an invaluable wide range of information on Standard English in practice and written communication.

Part 1

<u>Basic Grammar</u>

. <u>Introduction</u>

Words are essential for communication. Without applying the rules of grammar, the combination of words will result in a jumbled collection of words. The essence of grammar is that it has some rules for putting words together in recognised formats namely, phrases, clauses and sentences. Here we are concerned with the basic rules of grammar that enable us to put words in the right order and make our intended meaning clear. If the intended meaning is understood, you can rest assure that your grammar is all right. The following basic rules of grammar are essential for good writing.

. <u>Word classes(or parts of speech)</u>

Your vocabulary can be described as your stock of words. When you write or speak you draw words from your vocabulary. Sometimes you may consult a dictionary or ask someone for a particular word. For instance:

> . I speak with you.

In this sentence, each word can be labelled in terms of word classes: For example:

.<u>I</u> <u>speak</u> <u>with</u> <u>you</u>.
⇑ ⇑ ⇑   ⇑
1 **2** **3**   **4**

1 ⇒pronoun   2 ⇒verb   3 ⇒preposition   4 ⇒pronoun

Here is another example:

- **We tried hard but nowhere could we find the missing child**.

1⤶ 2⤶   3⤶ 4⤶   5⤶   6⤶ 7⤶ 8⤶   9⤶ 10⤶   11⤶

In this sentence:

      1 ⟹ pronoun   2 ⟹verb

      3 ⟹ adverb(it can be adjective)

      4 ⟹conjunction (it can be adverb, preposition or noun)

      5 ⟹ adverb   6 ⟹verb

      7 ⟹pronoun   8 ⟹verb

      9 ⟹ definite article or determiner

     10 ⟹ adjective   11 ⟹ noun

The above examples illustrate that a sentence can be analysed into its components known as word classes or parts of speech. It is a <u>word</u>, which is placed in a particular word class. **What is a word?**

A word is a single and independent unit(e.g. love) of vocabulary. It can be recognised in writing as well as in speech. Many words can be placed in more than one word class in accordance with their position in the **grammatical structure**.

• **The grammatical structure**

It is the way we arrange words by applying the rules of grammar into phrases, clauses and sentences. Before we discuss phrases, clauses and sentences, let's examine word classes.

At this stage, it is worth mentioning that if you consult, say, three grammar books, you may find that each book has different numbers of word classes. For our purpose, the following word classes are most appropriate.

Nouns

. **Why do we need nouns?** We require nouns for naming:

- . **people** - Jon, Jane, Clinton, Taylor
- . **places** - London, Berlin, Delhi, Paris
- . **animals** – zebra, tiger, elephant, fox, fish
- . **natural things** – earth, water, sun, wind, space, stars
- . **artefacts** - car, aeroplane, boat, computer, cloth
- . **abstracts** - hate, beauty, love, capitalism, liberty

Nouns make up the biggest category of word classes. The simple reason is that everything in this world whether tangible (bird) or intangible (honesty) is given a name.

. Noun types

The biggest word class namely noun has two types:

    . **Proper nouns**   . **Common nouns**

Some examples are listed in Table 1.

. How can you make a distinction between these two types of nouns?

You can see from the Table 1 that **proper nouns** are for specific things. These are names given to some unique place, person or whatever in this world. For instance, there is only one country in this world called **Egypt**. Similarly, **John** and **James** are two unique persons because they differ from each other in many ways.

On the other hand, **common nouns** describe things. They do not refer to any particular person, animal or whatever is concerned. For instance, the common noun **history** does not by itself refer to any particular event or event which happened in the past, except it gives a broad description of a turning point in the past. However, **Indian History** is not a common noun. It is a proper noun because it refers to the history of a unique place called India.

Types of nouns

Proper nouns	Common nouns
Germany	music
Egypt	capital
John	history
James	computer
Chelsea Club	hall
Winter	country
Waterloo	bicycle

Table 1

. Do we write proper and common nouns in different ways ?

Yes indeed, the proper noun begins with a capital letter whether a proper noun starts a sentence or not, e.g.

- **Anne** is already here.
- I wrote to a friend in **Nottingham** yesterday.
- We met on a train bound to **Budapest** some years ago.

. Is there any exception to this rule?

The exception to the above rule is that **seasons** do not begin with a capital letter unless they start a sentence. Here are some examples:

. **Winter** is already here.

starts the sentence↵

. During the **winter** months, we live in **Spain**.

proper noun↵   proper noun↵

. **Winter** ended about a month ago.

. Names of languages, nationalities and names of particular products are always written with an initial capital letter, e.g.

. Her mother language is **French**. She was born in France. It means she is **French**.

. Last year we bought a **Golf car**. It has a **Sony DVD 2003**.

. Concrete and abstract common nouns

Common nouns have their own two classes namely concrete and abstract. If we can see and touch something, we call it **tangible**. Tangible things(motor, computer, garden). are <u>concrete common nouns</u>.

Some examples of concrete and abstract common nouns

Concrete common nouns	Abstract common nouns
car	socialism
horse	happiness
man	fright
book	love
aeroplane	weakness
picture	opportunity
rail	freedom
coat	democracy
jumper	idea

Table 2

In this world, there are many ideas, concepts and qualities which do not have material existence because they are intangible(beauty, falsity, capitalism) and exist in our thought. These descriptive intangibles such as staff morale are known as <u>abstract common nouns</u>.

. Countable and uncountable nouns

For the development of good writing skills, it is important to understand the difference between the countable and uncountable nouns as follows:

. Countable nouns

Countable nouns have the following properties:

. they can be counted, e.g. four cows, twenty students

. they have both singular and plural forms, e.g.

woman $\Rightarrow$ singular and women $\Rightarrow$ plural

. they are usually preceded by a determiner, e.g.

. This is **a** car.

determiner↵ - see determiners

. She knows **every** member of her staff well.

determiner↵ - see determiners

. Uncountable (uncount or mass) nouns

These nouns have the following properties:

. They cannot be counted, e.g. equipment, light, happiness, sorrow, pride, sleep, steam

. They have only one singular form(no plural form), e.g.

information $\Rightarrow$ singular form.

For example:

. Our **information** is that he was arrested yesterday in France.

singular form ↵

In this example, **information** is the subject of the sentence and thus followed

by a singular **verb** $\Rightarrow$ **is** See $\Rightarrow$ sentences

. They can be used with or without a determiner, e.g.

. **The** equipment for the nursing department has arrived.

determiner↵ - (definite article) – see determiners

. This African tribe is threatened with **extinction**.

uncountable noun is not preceded by a determiner↵

. Some uncountable nouns are preceded by a **partitive phrase** or **word**,
  e.g. a piece of, two --- of, some----

Here are some examples of their use:

    . She has **a piece of** information for you.
partitive phrase↵
    . There is **some** jam left in that jar.
partitive word↵
     . We have **two items of** furniture which your wife ordered today.
     . Have you got **some** useful information for me?

. Some nouns can be either countable or uncountable

The following examples illustrate this property of some nouns:
    . Some of our ideas appear to be in **conflict** with each other.
                    uncountable noun↵
    . There is always a **conflict** between love and duty.
          countable noun↵ - it is preceded by the determiner **a**

. All citizens must have equal rights and **freedom** in a democratic country.
                    countable noun↵ - plural form
. He finally won his **freedom** after such a long court case.

     uncountable noun↵ ▬ single format

. Noun gender

Proper and common nouns have gender. The idea of gender is based on
male(man) and female(woman). The male is masculine and woman is
feminine gender. The **masculine** and **feminine** gender classification also applies to animals. Other things are placed in the third category called **neuter**.

. Are there any nouns which do not come under one particular gender group?

Some nouns can have a **dual gender**, e.g. student, nurse, teacher, doctor,
prime minister, dancer, etc.

Some examples of gender classification

Proper Nouns		
Masculine	**Feminine**	**Neuter**
Barry Black	Anne King	England
Elvis Presley	Sophia Daisy London	Paris
Muhammad Ali	Mary White	Virgin Airline
Alexander Berios	Elizabeth Taylor	American Express

Common Nouns		
Masculine	**Feminine**	**Neuter**
boy	girl	computer
man	woman	star
policeman	policewoman	post office
tiger	tigress	railway
stallion	mare	book

Table 3

. Singular and plural nouns

A <u>**singular noun**</u> refers to one of something, e.g. book, boat, letter.

A **plural noun** indicates that there are more than one thing, e.g. books, boats, letters. It is **a number** of things of the same kind. The difference between singular and plural nouns is expressed as '**number**'.

. How can we form plural nouns?

Most plural nouns are formed by changing the endings of singular nouns. This is demonstrated below:

1. lip ⇒singular **lips** ⇒plural formed by adding '**s**' to the ending of the
singular noun

2. gas⟹ singular **gases** ⟹plural formed by adding **'es'** to the ending
of the singular noun

3. body⟹singular **bodies** ⟹plural formed by changing **y** into **'ies'**

4. Most nouns follow the above rules. The problem is that there are some
irregular nouns which do not obey these rules.

    4a . Some irregular nouns form their plural by replacing their
ending **'f'** with **'ves'.** For instance:

        . **wife** ⟹ singular **wives** ⟹plural

        . **knife** ⟹ singular **knives**⟹plural

    4b . Some irregular nouns form their plural in some peculiar ways, e.g.

        . **tooth**⟹ singular **teeth**⟹plural

        . **goose**⟹ singular **geese**⟹plural

        . **woman**⟹ singular **women**⟹plural

5. Another very small group of nouns has two plural forms, e.g.

   . **appendix** ⟹singular **appendixes** or **appendices**⟹ two plural forms

 . **formula** ⟹singular **formulae** or **formulas**⟹ two plural forms

    6. Some nouns are really troublesome to a great many people because
they are inconsistent. Fortunately, there are not too many of these, e.g.

    . **scissors** ⟹plural noun but it is used with a phrase "a pair" as a
singular noun
        . This pair of scissors was bought in Rome.

   . **media** ⟹ plural form of the noun **medium**.
        Many people use it as plural only, but it is often used as a
singular noun, e.g.
        . The media **has** exaggerated this victory.

In fact, nouns in this group behave more like collective nouns which
often cause some confusion.

. Collective (or group) nouns

A collective noun refers to a group of people, animals or things, e.g. a club. A club has a number of people as members. It is, therefore, a collective noun. `There is some controversy surrounding the use of collective nouns, as they can be used with singular or plural verbs. Some people prefer to use only the plural verb after a collective noun. Indeed, some collective nouns can agree with only the plural verb. On the other hand, either singular or plural verbs can be used with a collective noun. This is illustrated below:

. Our **goods were delivered** yesterday by Parcel Force.

collective noun↵   ⇑

     plural form of the verb

The plural form of the verb always follows the collective noun **goods**, even if it represents only one item of something.

. Joan's **family is** in need of some urgent financial help.

family is taken as 'a single unit' ↵ ⇑

     singular verb form

. Joan's **family are** well off financially.

family is considered as 'a number individuals' ↵ ⇑

     plural verb form

. The committee **has/have** authorised the demolition of the derelict factory.

⇑

     use either singular/ plural verb form

Some collective nouns

Collective nouns	Collective nouns	Collective nouns
police	council	army
herd	class	flock
team	family	staff
committee	group	college
government	crowd	population

Table 4

Some compound nouns

Single words	Hyphenated words	A pair of words
Milkman	take-away	human rights
Postman	face–to-face	film star
housewife	low-cost	health food
motorway	father-figure	heart attack
teapot	baby-sitter	motor car
businessman	point-of-sale	air raid
shoplifting	pen-friend	wine bar
chairwoman	long-term	book token
semicircle	out-of-date	bank account
chairperson	cover-up	driving licence
motorcycle	bride-to-be	telephone number

Table 5

. Compound nouns

Two or more words make a compound noun. There are no hard and fast rules for writing compound nouns, as these may be written as 'single words', 'hyphenated words' or 'a pair of words'.

You may find that a particular compound noun in two or more dictionaries is not spelled in the same way. It is therefore, a good idea to be consistent with your own spelling of compound nouns. If in doubt, consult a quality diction- ary. Some compound nouns are shown in Table 5 above.

. Possessive forms of nouns

The possessive forms of nouns are used to express relationship, ownership or possession. For instance:

   1 . **Kim's sister** has arrived.

   2. **John's umbrella** is not here.

   3 . **Students' belongings** are locked up in a safe in our staff room.

. Examples 1-2 illustrate that in order to form a possessive noun when the noun is **singular** and it does not end with **'s', an apostrophe + s** is added to the singular noun.

. Example 3 indicates that to form **a** possessive noun from a plural noun ending in **s**, just add **an apostrophe** to the plural noun.

. How can you test that a word is a noun in a piece of writing?

One of the following tests can detect a noun:

. if there is a determiner in front of a noun, e.g. It is **a** pen.

. if a partitive phrase or word can be placed in front of a word, e.g.
    There is still **some** rain water in **the** loft.

. if a word indicates possession, relationship or ownership, e.g.
    John's car is parked in my place.

Pronouns

A pronoun is a word used as a substitute for a noun or noun phrase, e.g.

. **She** can talk faster than **you**.

pronoun⏎   pronoun⏎

There are different types of pronouns. Personal **pronouns** are used more frequently than any other type of pronoun.

. Pronoun types

Pronouns can be classified as discussed below.

. Personal and possessive pronouns

Personal pronouns identify persons and things without naming them, e.g. I, you, we, it. On the other hand, possessive pronouns denote that something belongs to someone. It does not mean that it is owned, but somehow is in the possession of someone, e.g. mine, ours, his, hers theirs.

Some people consider these as <u>possessive determiners</u> or just <u>determiners</u>. See Tables 6 and 7.

Let's consider the following examples:

. Do <u>**you**</u> like tea? Yes. I like <u>**it**</u>.

personal pronoun↵   personal pronoun↵ - refers to second person
second person   singular form
singular form -
it can be plural - second person

. Whose car is this? It is **mine**.

possessive pronoun↵ -refers to first person singular form

. <u>**I**</u> must go home now.

personal pronoun↵ - refers to first person singular form

. <u>**They**</u> were here five minutes ago.
⇑

personal pronoun - third person - plural form

. All personal pronouns refer to people, with the exception of **it**. It refers to animals or things.

. A subjective/subject pronoun occurs in the subject position in a clause/ sentence, if the pronoun is the subject, e.g.

. **He** loves <u>her</u>.

subject ↵ object↵

. An objective/object pronoun takes place in the objective position in a clause/sentence as illustrated above. It can be used alone, e.g.

. My employers wrote to **me**.

personal pronoun/ objective pronoun ↵

.Who can talk to him at this difficult time? – **Me**.

personal(objective/object) pronoun used alone ↵

. **One** – the indefinite pronoun can be used as a personal pronoun in order to refer to people in general, e.g.

. <u>**One**</u> should not be afraid of <u>**one's**</u> background.
⇑   ⇑

subjective pronoun - third person   possessive pronoun - in this case the
use of an apostrophe is 'exceptional'

<u>One</u> can be the subject as well as the object. When it is acting as an object, it
is a substitute for a possessive pronoun.

Personal pronouns

Number singular	Subjective(subject) Pronouns	Objective(object) Pronouns
First person	I	me
Second person	you	you
Third person	he, she, it	him, her, it
Number Plural		
First person	we	us
Second person	you	you
Third person	they	them

Table 6

Possessive pronouns

Number singular	Dependent form used with nouns*	Independent form used instead of nouns
First person	my	mine
Second person	your	yours
Third person	his, her, its	his, hers, its
Number Plural		
First person	our	ours
Second person	your	yours
Third person	their	theirs

Table 7

* possessive determiners/possessive adjectives (see below)*
. No apostrophe is needed when writing any of the above possessive
   pronouns, except in the case of one's as shown above.
. Possessive pronouns relates to possession of something.
.* Possessive pronouns are also known as possessive adjectives - when
   in front of a noun. They act as possessive determiners - when in front of a
   noun. For instance:
                              . **My** car is being serviced today.

Pronouns listed in Tables 6-7 occur more frequently in both spoken and
written English than any other type of pronouns.

. **Reflexive pronouns**

A reflexive pronoun refers back to the subject, e.g.

   . **She** made a nice cup of tea for **herself**.
        ⇑   ⇑
      subject   object
   personal pronoun   reflexive pronoun refers back to the subject

      . **Wolfgang** bought a suit for **himself** without telling Anne.
           ⇑   ⇑
        subject   object
         noun   reflexive pronoun refers back to the subject

Reflexive pronouns

Number	Singular	Plural
First person	myself	ourselves
Second person	yourself	yourselves
Third person	himself, herself, itself	themselves

Table 8

. Reflexive pronouns are helpful, when it is desired to emphasize the
   subject's action. When a reflexive pronoun is used in this way, it is known
   as an intensifying pronoun. For instance:

. Our parents constructed this house **themselves**.

placing emphasis on the subject's action↲

. This little girl dialled 999 **herself**, when her mother passed out.

. <u>Relative pronouns</u>

A relative pronoun links a subordinate clause to a main clause. There are only a few relative pronouns: **that, which, whom, whose, whose**.
Here are some examples:

. John got married to a rich woman **who** <u>helped him to set up his business.</u>

subordinate clause/relative clause↲ - see ⟹ sentences

. The house **that** we visited has been our family home for more than a century.

. Anne is Wolfgang's wife **who** goes to work on her moped.

<u>Nowadays an increasing number of people do not use **that**</u> – the relative pronoun, e.g.

. The house we visited has been our family home for more than a century.

. <u>Interrogative pronouns</u>

There are only five interrogative pronouns: **What, which, who, whom, whose**. Interrogative pronouns are also known as **wh-words**, because we use them for asking questions. For instance:

. **What** is the matter with you?
. **Which** of these colours would you prefer?

These pronouns also function as relative pronouns. See ⟹ relative pronouns

. <u>Reciprocal pronouns</u>

There are only two reciprocal pronouns. These are:

one another	each other

The pronoun **each other** refers to a relationship between two persons, whilst the pronoun **one another** states a link between more than two persons. The following examples illustrate the difference between the intended meanings communicated by these pronouns:

. Adam and Rachel visit **each other**.

Adam visits Rachel and Rachel visits Adam↵

. Students in my class work with **one another**.

each student helps the other student↵

. You can also use these pronouns to indicate possession, e.g.
. Anne and Wolfgang can drive **each other's** cars.
. Overseas students visits **one another's** homes on an exchange basis.
. They love each **other/one another** very much.

⇑

you can use any of the reciprocal pronouns with 'they'
because it can mean two persons or more.

. Demonstrative pronouns

There are only the following four demonstrative pronouns:

This	these	that	those

They are called demonstrative because they demonstrate something by way of pointing to a person or whatever. For example:

. **This** is my pen.

⇑ ⇒ singular form

it indicates that the pen is near to the speaker at this point in time

. **These** are my children.

⇑ ⇒ plural form

it points to children not far from the speaker

. **That** big man over there is our Member of Parliament.

⇑ ⇒ singular form

it indicates something (man) farther away - not too close to the speaker

. **Those** books were bought in Paris.

⇑ ⇒ plural form

it means books are farther away - not so near to the speaker

. Indefinite pronouns

An indefinite pronoun does not refer to a particular person or thing. There are a number of words which are used as indefinite pronouns to refer to people and things in general. Table 9 contains some common indefinite pronouns.

Indefinite pronouns

all	any	anyone	anything	another
both	each	either	everybody	everyone
few	least	less	little	many
much	neither	nobody	no one	nothing
one	several	somebody	someone	something

Table 9

. As highlighted in the above table, **no one** is the only pronoun which consists of two words. Some pronouns can also function as determiners and adverbs. Here are some examples to illustrate their application:

   . **Some** children are quicker than others.

   ⇈

   determiner- it is used here before a countable plural noun

   . The resolution was defeated as **some** voted against it.

                    pronoun↵ -used here for a number of people

. The word **neither** is an adverb, a determiner and a pronoun, e.g.

           . John did not attend the meeting and **neither** did I.

      an adverb - it is modifying the sentence adverb↵

           . **Neither** book is recommended for our course.

      determiner↵ - used before a noun **book**

           . **Neither** were returned back from the battlefield.

      pronoun↵

It is also used as a coordinating conjunction.

See ⇒ coordinating conjunction

           . Is **someone** at the door?

      pronoun ↵ - it means not mentioned by name or unknown

. Pronouns **all, little, some much, lot** are often used to express quantity. Here are some examples:

. We have eaten **all** of it.
. Please save a **little** for Alex.
. I must add that **much** has already been discussed.
. We invited 100 guests but **a lot** didn't come.

                    pronoun↵ - used instead of a noun
. We invited 100 guests but **a lot of** guests didn't come.
                    ⇑

    determiner - before a plural noun to quantify it - a large number
. **It is a good idea to avoid using a pronoun if you can use a noun
  or noun phrase instead. This way you can prevent any possible
  misunderstanding, e.g.**

. If your car is costing you too much money to run on this petrol, change **it**.

              it is somewhat confusing – it can mean car or petrol↵

Instead of '**change it**', try '**change this petrol**', as it is the petrol that is too
expensive for you. Is it still clumsy? It is best to re-write the sentence.

Adjectives

We use an adjective to compare the quality of something with the quality of
some other thing(s) <u>of the same kind</u>. In doing so, the main function of an
adjective is to define or modify the noun or the pronoun. In this context, the
word modify means to describe or limit the meaning of a noun or pronoun in
some way. Adjectives enable us to make comparison For instance:

        . I thought she was a **<u>small</u>** but **<u>young</u>** lady.
          adjective 1↵adjective 2↵
                              noun

In this sentence, both adjectives are describing a lady in terms of her physical
size and age. This way, these adjectives have placed a limit on her body and
her age. This is what we mean by modifying or qualifying the noun or pronoun. In this case, the noun **lady** is modified by two adjectives. Here is another example:

. It is really an **expensive** jacket for me.

      adjective↵

These examples illustrate that an adjective can occur before a noun or pronoun. When an adjective comes before a noun/pronoun, it is called an **attributive adjective**. An attributive adjective tells us about the attribute of
the noun.

    . I am **tired** tonight.

  adjective ↵ - giving further information about the subject - I am

    . Marry is **well** now.

    adjective ↵ - giving further information about the subject - Mary

In the last two examples, adjectives occur in the predicate (not before the
noun). The predicate is that part of the sentence /clause that comes after the
verb. See Phrases, Clauses and Sentences.

When an adjective occurs in the predicate, it is called a **predicative adjective**. In each example, the adjective is giving us some information about the
subject, but after the verb of each sentence.

. Most adjectives can be placed in both attributive and predicative positions.
It is worth mentioning that there are some adjectives that can be used in
one particular position. For instance, **maximum, introductory, woollen,
underlying** and **neighbouring** are adjectives that can occur only in the
attributive position. The following examples illustrate their usage.

    . The **maximum** fine is £1000.
    . It is an **introductory** chapter.
    . Lancashire is the **neighbouring** county.
    . The **underlying** message is that our company is in financial trouble.
    . It was a **woollen** mill.

. On the other hand, **allergic, subject, full, aware** and **parallel** are among
those adjectives which are usually used in the **predicative position only**.
For example:

    . Amanda is **allergic** to nuts. ⇐ **allergic** is always followed by **to**
  . Poor people are more **subject** to heart attack than affluent people*.

    always followed by to↵

* except those affluent people who are alcoholic

. The bucket is **full** of rain water. ⇐ **full** is always followed by **of**
                                    when it refers to space or
                                    having a lot of something
        . She is not really **aware** of the problem.
always followed by of↵
        . The Market Street and the railway line are **parallel** to each other.
                            always followed by to↵

. Adjective forms

The good thing about adjectives is that they can be graded in order to show
the extent of quality, size, age, colour or whatever is being said about something. The basic form of adjectives is the one which is listed in dictionaries.
This form is called **descriptive (or positive)**. Here are some adjectives in
their descriptive form:

sad, beautiful, small, large, easy, loud, poor, tall

Adjectives enable us to make comparisons between two or more things or
whatever. When we use an adjective for comparing two things, we use the
comparative form of the adjective. The comparative form of the adjective
is derived from its descriptive form. For instance:

        . tall ⇒ descriptive form **taller** ⇒ comparative form
          e.g.
        . John is **taller** than Sam.

        . ugly ⇒ descriptive form **uglier** ⇒ comparative form
          e.g.
        . Joan is **uglier** than me.

. There are occasions when you want to compare more than two people, etc.
   For this purpose, we use the **superlative form** of the adjective, e.g.
        . poor ⇒ descriptive form **poorer** ⇒ comparative form **poorest**
                                            superlative form
        . This is the **poorest district** in our town.
                            ⇑
        the superlative form is telling us that there is no other district
        as poor as this one.

. How do we form comparative and superlative adjectives?

Most adjectives have regular forms. The regular forms mean that the comparative and superlative forms are derived from the descriptive adjectives in accordance with the following rules for forming the **comparative form**:
> . add **'-er'** to the end of the descriptive adjective, **or**
> . place **'more'** in front of the descriptive adjective

See Table 11 for example

. To form the superlative regular form, apply the following rules:

> . Add **'-est'** to the end of the descriptive adjective, **or**
> . place **'most'** in front of the descriptive adjective

See Table 11 for example

. Irregular forms

There are a great many adjectives that have regular forms. On the other hand, there are some other adjectives that have **irregular forms**.

It means that in order to form their comparative and superlative forms, there are no hard and fast rules to apply. For instance, **good** and **bad** are two such adjectives. Table 10 contains some irregular adjectives and their respective comparative and superlative forms.

Some irregular adjectives

Descriptive	Comparative	Superlative
bad	worse	worst
good	better	best
far	farther or further	farthest or furthest

Table 10

. Long and short adjectives

. Do we have to make some spelling changes before adding **'-er'** and **'-est'** to the descriptive adjectives to form comparative and superlative adjectives?

Yes. Before you can add either **'-er'** or **'-est'** to some descriptive adjectives, you have to change the end of the adjective in accordance with the following rules:
    . The spelling of an adjective tells us if it is one-syllable, two-syllable

In fact, not all descriptive adjectives take **'-er'** or **'est'** to form their respective comparative and superlative adjectives. Such adjectives have irregular forms.

Three forms of some regular adjectives

Descriptive	Comparative	Superlative
broad	broader	broadest
cold	colder	coldest
few	fewer	fewest
great	greater	greatest
long	longer	longest
loud	louder	loudest
narrow	narrower	narrowest
sharp	sharper	sharpest
short	shorter	shortest
small	smaller	smallest
strong	stronger	strongest
beautiful	more beautiful	most beautiful
difficult	more difficult	most difficult
exclusive	more exclusive	most exclusive
intelligent	more intelligent	most intelligent

Table 11

. Is it possible to recognise a word as an adjective?

There are thousands of adjectives. Initially, many of these words were not adjectives. They were either nouns or verbs. With the passage of time, a great many number of words became adjectives. The endings of words shown in Table 12 can enable you to decide, if a particular word is an adjective or not.

It should be remembered that a word can be placed in a number of word classes (parts of speech). Some words end with –y and –ly and can be both adjectives and adverbs. For instance:

. **weekly** $\Rightarrow$ is both an adjective and an adverb
          (it can also be a part of a name, e.g. weekly magazine)

. **very** $\Rightarrow$ is both an adjective and an adverb

. A word ending with –**y** or –**ly** can only be an adjective or an adverb, e.g.

  . **thankfully** $\Rightarrow$ is an adverb only   . **funny** $\Rightarrow$ is an adjective only

These examples illustrate that words which end with –**ly** and –**y** can cause some confusion when you want to use them correctly.

Word ending guide for the recognition of adjectives

Word ending	Adjectives	Word ending	adjectives
able	fashionable, comparable,---	ing	charming, tiring,---
al	brutal, mortal,---	ish	childish, squeamish,---
ar	popular, singular,---	ive	defensive, offensive,---
ed	intimidated, excited, ---	less	helpless, harmless,---
ent	intelligent, excellent, ---	like	businesslike, warlike,---
ful	hopeful, wonderful,---	ous	famous, notorious,---
ible	impossible, unintelligible, ---	some	handsome, tiresome,--
ic	classic, dramatic, ---	worthy	roadworthy, trust-worthy,---

Table 12

. Intensifiers

Adjectives can be graded by means of **intensifiers**. The purpose of placing an intensifier in front of an adjective is to modify the quality referred to by an adjective. For this reason, intensifiers are also known as **sub-modifiers**. In fact, an adjective modifies the noun by attaching a quality to it, e.g.

    . Mr Brown is a **very kind** person.

In this example, the intensifier **very** is intensifying the quality described by the adjective **kind** of the **person** who is Mr. Brown. This way, the intensifier is functioning as a submodifier. The intensifier **very** upgraded the quality referred to by the adjective **kind**.

There are some intensifiers that precede the adjective in order to reduce the quality of an adjective, e.g.

    . My husband is **quite a tall** man.

In the last example, the intensifier has the effect of reducing the height, as '**quite**' means not exactly or somewhat less. Here are some more intensifiers:

---

almost, amazing, bitterly, entirely, extremely, fairly, a good deal(in front of comparative adjectives), a great deal(in front of comparative adjectives), highly, hopelessly, a lot (in front of comparative adjectives),moderately, much, nearly, really, reasonably, remarkably, pretty, somewhat, terribly, very.

. Often people say, 'I am **too** happy to see you.'

        incorrect use↵

   too cannot be used instead of the intensifier ⇒ **very**

. It should be written/spoken as: 'I am **very** happy to see you.'

It is important to remember that an adjective can be identified by its position in either attributive or predicative and its ability to be graded. Adjectives are almost always used with a noun or pronoun, as shown above. However, there are occasions when adjectives also come after a linking verb, e.g.

     . I became ill.

   linking verb↵ - ill ⇒adjective

Verbs

It is necessary for us to express present, past and future actions and states. We do so by using verbs. Like noun class, verb class plays a pivotal role in both speech and writing. You cannot express an **action**, describe a **state** or **condition** without a verb. In fact, you cannot construct a clause or a sentence without a verb. For instance:

. I <u>walk</u> everyday in the morning.

verb indicating action↵

        . She <u>feels</u> cold now.

verb indicating state /condition↵

There are many thousands of words that are classed as verbs. Verbs also indicate time that is called **tense**, e.g.

    . **present tense:** I go.
    . **past tense:**   I went.
    . **future tense:** I will go.

See ⟹ Tenses

Verbs are most commonly used words in writing. It is important to understand their forms, types, classes and attributes, and how you, as a writer, can put them into practice.

. <u>Verb forms</u>

Verbs can be recognised by their following four distinct forms:

> . **Base form** - it is also known as **bare infinitive**, **root form** or **stem**. You can find this type in dictionaries because verbs are listed in this form. Here are some verbs in their base form:

> **love, hate, look, see, speak, want, wish, promise, dance**

Often the base form is preceded by the word 'to' in order to form **to-infinitive**, e.g. to cook, to prepare, to work, etc. Here the function of 'to' is to act as **to-infinitive marker.** The word **to** with the base form of the verb (**to** walk) is also known as **particle**.

> . **s/es form** — the base form is changed that is often called **inflected**, when the verb is used with the third person singular of the subject by adding '**-s**' or '**-es**', e.g.
> > . **She <u>loves</u>** her children very much.

subject third person singular↵   ⇑

        base form of the **verb** love is inflected by adding '**s**' to it

. **Present participle form** — the ending of the base form of a verb is extended by adding '**ing**'. In some cases, the ending of the base form has to be changed before adding '**ing**'. It is illustrated by the following examples:

base form	present participle form
go	go**ing** (+ ing)
work	work**ing** (+ ing)
love	lov**ing** (base form changed + ing)
become	becom**ing** (base form changed + ing)
run	runn**ing** (base form changed + ing)
smoke	smok**ing** (base form changed + ing)

There is no rule that can be applied to many thousands of verbs and how to inflect these into participle forms. The best rule is to learn each verb and its participle form. Here are some examples of using the participle form:

> . I am **going** home.
> . She has been **smoking** since she was a college student.
> . Angelica is **running** to catch a bus.

. Past participle form

(1) . regular verbs – the ending of
   the base form of a verb is inflected to become '**ed**', e.g.

base form	past participle form
cover	covered
turn	turned
laugh	laughed
clear	cleared

(2) . irregular verbs – the ending of the base form of verbs is inflected to become 'en', 'some other endings', 'change of spelling', 'changing of spelling plus en' or 'no change' takes place, e.g.

The **verb inflection** takes place in accordance with the function a verb is going to perform.

. Regular and irregular verbs

Verbs are divided into two groups:

. **<u>Regular verbs</u>**

The majority of verbs are regular verbs. These verbs are also known as **weak verbs** because they change their forms in a predicted pattern to express tense or time. Table 14 contains some regular verbs.

. **<u>Irregular verbs</u>**

Out of several thousands of verbs, only about **300** verbs are irregular verbs. Some of these are shown in Tables 13 and 15. These verbs are also known as **strong verbs**, as they do not change their forms in a regular pattern to express tense or time.

<u>Some irregular verbs and their conversion to their past participle forms</u>

Base Form	Past participle form	changing of the base form
become	became	spelling changed
break	broken	spelling changed+ en
fall	fallen	+en
stink	stunk/stank	spelling changed
weep	wept	spelling changed
lead	led	spelling changed
hurt	hurt	no change
hit	hit	no change
shut	shut	no change
withdraw	withdrawn	+n

<u>Table 13</u>

. <u>Verb classes</u>

Verbs shown in Tables 13 - 15 are **<u>main or lexical</u>** verbs. Some people also call these verbs **<u>ordinary verbs</u>**. These verbs arc lexical because they are relating to vocabulary in the English language. They constitute the main body of verbs in English. **Read on Page 33**.

Some Regular Verbs

Base form	Present form 's/es' added to the base form	Participle form 'ing' added to the base form	Past participle form 'ed' to the base form
act	acts	acting	acted
blame	blames	blaming	blamed
complete	completes	completing	completed
concern	concerns	concerning	concerned
correct	corrects	correcting	corrected
enter	enters	entering	entered
establish	establishes	establishing	established
look	looks	looking	looked
miss	misses	missing	missed
visit	visits	visiting	visited

Table 14

Some Irregular Verbs

Base Form	Present Form	Participle form	Past participle form
begin	begins	beginning	began/begun
bend	bends	bending	bent
drink	drinks	drinking	drank/drunk
freeze	freezes	freezing	frozen
hide	hides	hiding	hidden
ride	rides	riding	ridden
see	sees	seeing	seen
shake	shakes	shaking	shaken
swim	swims	swimming	swam/swum
weep	weeps	weeping	wept
write	writes	writing	wrote/written

Table 15

A smaller number of verbs, which are used with main verbs are called **auxiliary verbs**. Auxiliary verbs work with main verbs to express a very wide range of meanings that is almost beyond one's imagination.

. **Auxiliary Verbs** - these verbs are also divided into the primary and
            modal auxiliaries:
    . **primary auxiliaries:** 'be', 'do' and 'have'. These are
                illustrated below:
        . A student **is being interviewed** by the tutor.
        primary auxiliary verb⏎   ⇑
                    main/lexical/ordinary verb
        . He **has done** his homework already.
    primary auxiliary verb⏎   ⇑
            main/lexical/ordinary verb
        . Adam **had served** as a soldier in Bosnia.
        primary auxiliary verb⏎   ⇑
                main/lexical/ordinary verb
. The negative forms are formed by <u>adding **not, e.g.**</u>

            . She **is not taking** part in this competition.
    primary auxiliary negative form⏎   ⇑
            main/lexical/ordinary verb

. The primary auxiliaries 'be', 'do', 'have' have different forms that are used
  in tenses in accordance with the subject singular, plural and gender
  classification. These are summarized in Table 16.
        . **Modal auxiliaries:**
                can, could, may, might, shall,
                should, will, would, ought to,
                dare, must and need

Modal auxiliary verbs enable us to express our moods or attitudes in both writing and speech. Like the primary auxiliary verbs, modal auxiliaries help the main verb in expressing a wide range of meanings. The following examples demonstrate the range of meanings express by modal auxiliaries:

. She **can** swim. ⇐ ability

. **Can** I leave now? ⇐ permission

. He **cannot** play the piano. ⇐ inability

. Brunel **could** design buildings when he was still a child. ⇐ ability

. The teacher said, 'You **could** submit your project one week later than
   the due date.' ⇐ permission

. Our sales are declining so much that we **could** be closing down
   the business.   ⇐ permission/forecast/prediction

. You **could** at least telephone me from the rail station. ⇐ suggestion

. **Could** you please close the window? ⇐ request/politely asking

. **May I** ask you a question? ⇐ permission

. I **might** be able to help you. ⇐ possibility

. I **must** interview some applicants for the job this morning. ⇐ necessity

. I **will** join you for a lunch at 13 hours in our staff restaurant. ⇐ intention

. We **would** help you financially, if we had some money
   to spare. ⇐ condition/forecast/prediction

. I **shall** play tennis tonight. ⇐ intention

. We **should** come back home by 20 hours tonight. ⇐ prediction

. We **ought** to invite them for lunch. ⇐ obligation/necessity

. I **daren't** disturb the board meeting. ⇐ not having enough courage

As a modal verb it is used in negative forms and in the present tense. Since
dare is also an ordinary word, it is discussed under Troublesome Words and
Phrases. Note that 'dare say' is an idiomatic expression, e.g. **I dare say**.

See ⇒ Troublesome Words and Phrases

. **Transitive and intransitive verbs**

These are ordinary verbs. It is important to understand the difference between
these two groups of verbs.

> . **A transit verb** - a transitive verb **cannot** stand alone. It must
>   have an object. The object can be a noun, a
>   pronoun, a noun phrase or a clause, e.g.

. You should **avoid** **him**.

transitive verb↵

object - pronoun

. We will **discuss** **this** report at the next meeting.

transitive verb↵

object - noun phrase

. **An intransitive verb** - it can stand alone without the object. Sometimes it can be followed a prepositional phrase, e.g.

. She **cried**.

. It **vanished**.

. They **arrived** by a taxi.

prepositional phrase↵

• Some regular verbs can function as transitive or intransitive, e.g.

. John has finished **the job**.

object ↵ - finished = transitive verb

. It is **finished**.

intransitive verb – no object needed

. Linking or copular or copula verbs

The Latin word '**copula**' means bond. This is the task of copula or linking verbs to bond or link the subject with a complement, e.g.

. It **is** my class.

. He **appeared** calm.

. We **remained** silent throughout the court hearing.

. She **became** a doctor.

. She **seems to** be very nice person.

In these examples, the linking verbs are shown in **bold style**. What follows the linking verb is the complement.

. There are only a few linking verbs. The most commonly used linking verb is '**be**' and its other forms are: **am, is, are, was, were**

. Participles

By now you know the meaning of present and past participles. The fact is that participles **cannot** function in their own rights as verbs. To make a participle work as a past participle verb, you must use it with an auxiliary verb, e.g.

> . She <u>is</u> dancing.

   auxiliary verb⤶

auxiliary verb+ present participle = present participle verb
> . She <u>has</u> danced.

   auxiliary verb⤶

 auxiliary verb+ past participle = past participle verb

On the other hand:

> . She <u>danced</u> all night at a wild party.
>
> ⇑

   past tense form of the verb dance

It is true to say that it is the past participle form of the verb dance, but it does not meet the criterion for functioning as a past participle verb.

<u>This example highlights the problem associated with participles that can function in more than one way.</u>

. Verbals and gerunds

This leads to the idea of **verbals**. A verbal is derived from a verb but it is <u>not used as a verb</u>. When the **'-ing'** form of the participle is used in a clause or a sentence, it can function either as a verbal noun or a verbal adjective. In another grammar book, these verbals may have some other names such as **'-ing' nouns** and **'-ing' adjectives,** For instance:

> . Have you got any qualifications in **computing**? ⇐ verbal noun

> . This statement is very **annoying**. ⇐ verbal adjective

The <u>**to-infinitive**</u> verbs can also function in phrases as verbals, e.g.

> . She telephoned her husband <u>**to break** the news of their child's birth.</u>
> . We all hoped <u>**to become** the winner of the National Lottery.</u>

In these examples phrases are underlined and verbals are printed in **bold style**.
. <u>When a verbal or participle verb formed with '**-ing**', is used on its own, in a phrase or in a clause as a noun, it is called a **gerund**.</u>

In the following examples, gerunds are shown in **bold style**:

       . **running** - ⇐ gerund by itself
       . Sara likes **dancing** very much.
       . You must come <u>to the **meeting** to night</u>.

               in a phrase↵
       . Daniel likes **running**.
       . It is rather difficult <u>not **walking** for a whole day</u>.

          with a negative in a phrase↵
       . Do you mind **waiting** <u>a moment by the reception desk</u> ?

in a question - forming a phrase↵

       . She said, '<u>It might be worth **taking** a taxi.</u>'
            in a clause ↵
       . I like <u>Ann's</u> **singing** very much.
possessive noun↵

A gerund can be modified by a possessive noun or pronoun. Therefore, **'Anne singing' would be incorrect.**

A gerund can be used in a wide range of situations, expressing a variety of meanings, when it is a component of different kinds of phrases and clauses.

. <u>Split infinitives</u>

If the verb is '**to-infinitive**' and you place a word or words (e.g. adverbs) between **to** and the **verb**, you create a split infinitive, e.g.

         . We are trying hard <u>to **really** help</u> you financially.

      split infinitive caused by really↵
         . <u>To **fully** understand</u> your report, we must read it.

split infinitive caused by fully↵

Both **really** and **fully** are adverbs.

Some people dislike the use of split infinitives and thus consider it incorrect.

. Phrasal verbs

A special group of verbs consists of many verbs (ordinary verbs) which are
called phrasal verbs. Each phrasal verb has more than one word in it.
Here are some phrasal verbs:

abide by, band together, climb down (over something), come forward,
dispose of, keep up with, let out, make away with/off(with), run up
against, vote out, write off, etc.

The overall meaning of a phrasal verb differs from the meanings of individual words that constitute it. For instance:

. As members of this club, we should **abide by** the rules of this club.

accept and act in accordance↲
. We have **to abide by** the terms and conditions of this loan agreement.

⇑

obey the terms and conditions
. Some people **came forward** to search for the missing child.

help offered↲
. We should keep this to ourselves – don't **let it out** to the press.

keep secret ↲ -information secret

A phrasal verb can be made of a verb and an adverb or a preposition. Some
phrasal verbs can have both an adverb and a preposition with a verb. Many
phrasal verbs are used only in informal contexts. It is, therefore, important to
learn not only the meaning of a phrasal verb but also the context in which it
is appropriate to use it. Many phrasal verbs can be used to express different
meanings in varied situations.

. Verbs in idioms

There is another very important body of expressions connected with verbs
which is known as **idioms**. An idiom is an expression which consists of some
words whose overall meaning cannot be predicted from the individual words
that constitute it. It must be emphasized that **not all idioms have verbs in
them**, **whilst all phrasal verbs contain verbs**. For instance:

. **in the air** – it is used when people know something is
happening or about to happen, e.g.

. It is almost the end of February. Well, the spring is **in the air**.

idiom without a verb in it ↵

. **hang in the air** – when some people avoid answering a question.
It may be that either they do not know the answer
or do not wish to get involved, e.g.

. At the public meeting, I asked the prime minister about the closure
of our local hospital. He talked at length, but left the question
hanging in the air.

idiom contains a verb ↵

Both idioms and phrasal verbs should be used without changing them. The
use of both idioms and phrasal verbs can make writing interesting, providing
the correct style is used. For instance, if an idiom or phrasal verb is considered as 'informal', it would be incorrect to use it in a formal letter. Here is a
useful reference for you:

Explore Essential English – Grammar, Structure & Style of Good English
Mark Slim
ISBN 190 1197 123
Published by A. D. R.(London) Limited in 2003

It contains over **1000** examples of idiomatic expressions with explanations
and examples of their usage. The author has also outlined some of the difficulties of locating idioms and styles of idiomatic expressions. It also points
that sometimes it is not easy to distinguish between an idiom and a phrasal
verb.

If you are enthusiastic about idiomatic expressions, please get a copy of this
title.

Different forms of primary auxiliary verbs

auxiliary ⇒ tense ⇓	be	do	have
Simple present tense	I am, you are we are they are he/she/it is	I do you do we do they do he/she/it does	I have you have we have they have he/she/it has
Simple past tense	I was you were we were they were he/she/it was	I did you did we did they did he/she/it did	I had you had we had they had he/she/it had

participles:-
    present ⇒
 	
    past ⇒
	being
	
	been
		doing
		
		done
			having
			
			had

Table 16

Adverbs

In both speech and writing, verbs help us to express action, state or condition. Adjectives add further information to the statement describing the state or action. Like adjectives, adverbs can enhance the meaning intended by the statement.

In both speech and writing, verbs help us to express action, state or condition. Adjectives add further information to the statement describing the state or action. Like adjectives, adverbs can enhance the meaning intended by the statement.

Sometimes it is not easy to distinguish an adverb from an adjective. In fact, a word can be placed in more than one word class, depending how it is used and its position in the statement. There are a great many adverbs. Here are some words that can be used as adverbs.

> about, after, afterwards, almost, always, around, abruptly,
> aggressively, again, barely, continually, clearly, enough, highly, just,
> lately, never, nervously, now, often, slowly, shortly, so, sometimes,
> there, too, truthfully, usually, weekly, monthly, yearly, widely, worriedly

The main function of an adverb is to modify or qualify a verb, another adverb, an adjective, adverbial phrase, prepositional phrase and conjunctions.

. **How can you use adverbs?**
. **Where can you place an adverb in a statement?**

. Adverbs are used in a variety of ways. Their use can be described under the
. **main types of adverbs** as described below:

. **Adverb of place** – an adverb of place informs us <u>where</u>
            something happens, happened or will occur, e.g.
    . My car is parked over <u>there</u>.
            adverb ↵ - modifying the verb ⟹ is parked
    . It is detailed <u>below</u>.
           adverb ↵ - modifying the verb ⟹ detailed
    . It must be kept <u>somewhere</u> in the house.
           adverb ↵ - modifying the verb ⟹ be kept

. **Adverb of time** – it tells <u>when</u> something happens happened or
            will take place, e.g.

. Our guests will arrive <u>**soon**</u>.

                adverb ↵ - modifying the verb ⟹ will arrive

. This meeting tapes place **weekly**.

. **<u>Adverb of manner</u>** – It is connected with **how** an event or
                      situation happens, e.g.

   . She speaks German <u>correctly</u>.

             adverb ↵ - it answers: how fluent is she in German?

   . Please tell us <u>honestly</u> about your last ten days.

   . We are talking happily.

   . A motorist just now <u>accidentally</u> killed our neighbour's cat.

   . It is a <u>properly</u> organised function.

. **<u>Adverb of frequency</u>** – it tells how many times an occurrence of
                      some event or situation takes place, e.g.

   . My grandfather **<u>never</u>** travelled abroad.

             adverb ↵ - it answers: how many times?

   . I met her **once** at her brother's wedding.

   . I see him at work **almost** everyday.

   . Babies grow **<u>day-by-day</u>**.

            adverb ↵ - gradually

. **<u>Adverb of degree</u>** – it shows the extent to which something is
                    performed, e.g.

   . Amanda admires her son <u>immensely</u>.

   . I am <u>somewhat</u> surprised to learn that he has resigned.

   . Barbara <u>absolutely</u> agrees with me.

   adverb of degree ↵ - emphasizing - it comes in front of the verb

        . We **<u>really</u>** like to eat at your restaurant.

adverb of degree ↵- emphasizing - it comes in front of the verb

. <u>Some adverbs (not many) are placed in front of the verb as illustrated by</u>
   <u>the last two examples.</u>

    . I know him **<u>better</u>** than my wife.

              ⇑

It is functioning as an **adverb of degree**

Note that **good**, **better**, **best** can be adjectives, nouns or adverbs.

. **<u>Adverb of reason and purpose</u>** – it tells us **why** something has happened, e.g.

- . He is using foul language. He is **obviously** drunk.
- . **Certainly**, early retirement means loss of regular income from work or business.
- . She has been **deliberately** ignoring him this evening because he forgot to bring some flowers for her.

. **<u>Adverb of viewpoint</u>** – it indicates a particular view regarding some action or state about something, e.g.

- . Our country cannot **financially** aid all poor countries in the world.
- . I, **personally**, do not think this is a workable plan.
- . Most financial journalists predict that China will soon become **economically** a great world power.

. **<u>Adverb of focus</u>** – it is used when the writer wants to pinpoint a word or phrase, e.g.

- . She used to telephone her mother **<u>every</u>** <u>night for the last ten years</u>.

adverb every used here to highlight the phrase↵   phrase↵

- . Please drive **<u>carefully</u>**.

pinpointing drive↵

- . The Channel Four News programme is broadcast **nightly**.

. **<u>Adverb of attitude</u>** – it indicates different attitudes such as someone's likes or dislikes, truth and other behavioural and relationship aspects, e.g.

- . 'Are you really a doctor?' I asked her **<u>curiously</u>**.

indicating a desire to know more about a particular person ↵

- . Not **surprisingly** on such a wonderful winter afternoon, our promenade is crowded with so many day-trippers.
- . I **honestly** like this place.

. **<u>Adverb for linking</u>** – it links previous thought or statement, e.g.

- . **Anyway**, Daniel lives in another part of the country.
- . There is little chance that the corner shop is open. **Nevertheless**, we must go by car and try to get a loaf.

. She likes staying at home most evenings. **Besides**, her son has just
returned from overseas.

. Position of an adverb

The examples given above demonstrate that adverbs can be placed or posi-
tioned at the beginning, in the middle or at the end of a sentence. Generally,
an adverb should be placed before the word it is modifying. In reality, this
rule does not always apply. For instance, the position of the adverb **'really'**
can change the meaning of the sentence:

. I **really** know that she loves you.

it means 'I am sure ↵ - it is modifying the verb ⟹ **know**

. I know that she **really** loves you.

it is modifying the verb loves ↵

It means 'I know that she certainly loves you' – emphasis is on
'she definitely loves you' **(definitely = really)**

These two examples further illustrate that the rule does not always work. The
best rule is to make sure that it is placed in its appropriate place in the context
in which it is used.

. How do you know if a word is an adverb or an adjective in a statement?

There are many adjectives and adverbs, which have the same form,
e.g. **fast**, **full**, **late**, **long**, **next**, **never**, **straight**, **well**, etc.

These words and many other such words can function either as adjectives or
adverbs, depending on the context in which they are used.

Many adjectives and adverbs have similar endings, e.g. '**-y**', '**-ly**', e.g.

. easy ⟹Adjective   . easily ⟹ **adverb**

Some other adjectives and adverbs have dissimilar endings, e.g.

. glorious ⟹ adjective   . gloriously ⟹adverb

. serious ⟹adjective   . seriously ⟹ adverb

. lucky ⟹adjective   . luckily ⟹adverb

. basic ⟹ adjective   . basically ⟹adverb

Adjectives and adverbs have the same function that is to add further information to the overall meaning of a statement. They do so by modifying or qualifying a word or a phrase. In spite of these similarities and dissimilarities, you can still deduct whether the word adding further information is an adjective or an adverb. For instance:

> . I am not a **well** person.
>
> adjective↵ modifying the noun ⇒person
>
> . I am not **well**.
>
> adverb↵ modifying the verb ⇒ 'be' in the form of 'am'

It is desirable to learn words and how they can function in a variety of context. Indeed, adverbs enhance the intended meaning and can make writing more interesting. Nevertheless, you can still write a sentence without a verb, which is grammatically correct and makes sense. However, it must be emphasized that sometimes it is better to include an adverb, e.g.

> . He said that he would love her **for ever/ always**.

This sentence without either of these adverbs would be less interesting. Of course, you can replace **for ever/always** by **all the time/ every time**.

Prepositions

There are a large number of prepositions in English. Most prepositions are simple or a single word, but there are some that consist of more than one word. Thus, a preposition can be a simple word or a group preposition. For instance:

Simple prepositions: about, above, among, around, at, between, by, circa, down, during, for, in, off, on, over, past round, since, towards, under, until, up, with, without, within, ...

Group prepositions: according to, ahead of, all over, because of, in accordance with, in front of, for the sake of, on behalf of, on top of, with reference to,...

Group prepositions are listed in some dictionaries as idioms.

Prepositions are used to link one part of a statement with another. This way, a preposition can indicate the relation of a noun, pronoun, noun phrase or clause to the other components of a statement.

In the following example, the whole statement is analysed in order to separate its two parts, and show that the preposition 'to' is linking one part with another part. In doing so, the preposition shows the relation between these two parts of this statement.

. **I travelled** to **Italy with my mother**.

part a ↵   ⇑   part b↵

preposition

Here is another example: . Brighton is **near** London.

preposition↵

In this case, it shows the relationship of London(noun) with the rest of the statement. Prepositions are really helpful in indicating all kinds of relationships.

. Preposition of place

The above examples illustrate that prepositions express a relationship of place because in both cases, the noun and the phrase refer to places.
Here are some more examples:

. My car is parked **in front of** your house.

preposition of place↵   place ↵

. The customer Parcel Collection Point is **next to** Bridlington
Post Office.
. Scotland is **beyond** Carlisle –the last English town.

. Preposition of time

It relates to time, e.g.

. We will arrive **about** 16.00 hours.
. I will not leave my office **until** I have finished this job.
. My parcel will arrive from Japan **in** the next few day.

. **At** the moment, I am not sure **about** my next move

prepositional phrase↵ - preposition ⟹ **at**

. We hope to start our new business **on** next Friday.

prepositional phrase↵ - preposition ⟹ **on**

. You can express time without a preposition. Instead of a preposition, use any of the following words:

every, last, later, next, this, tomorrow ,while, yesterday. For instance:

. I returned home **yesterday**.
. I was waiting **for** you for thirty minutes by the booking office.
. **During** the next two weeks, I will be in Moscow for my business.
. They were burgled **while** they were asleep.

during the sleeping time↵ - while ⟹conjunction

. Preposition of some other meanings

These are exemplified below:

. We came late **because of** torrential rain on the motorway.

preposition of reason/cause ↵ - but because is ⟹conjunction

. This year our company will not give us a salary increase **due to** poor sales.

preposition of reason/cause ↵

. My wife was **with** me most of the time when I was in hospital.

preposition of support ↵

. A member **of** our team is still missing.

preposition of possession↵

. He is intelligent **apart from** his mannerism.

preposition of attitude↵ - some other people may like his mannerism

. It is **up to** them to make their own travel arrangements.

⇑

preposition of responsibility

. Many people are **against** the government's educational cuts.

preposition of opposition↵

These examples illustrate that there are both simple and group prepositions for almost all kinds of occasions in order to indicate a very wide range of meanings.

. **Prepositions in idioms and phrasal verbs**

Many prepositions are part of both idioms and phrasal verbs, e.g.

. We must explore all avenues **for the sake of** peace in our country.

prepositions **for** and **of** in the idiom ↵

. **In accordance with** our agreement, I send you our payment.

idiom contains prepositions↵

. What time do you normally **get up**?

it is a phrasal verb and **up** is a preposition↵

. Our publicity has **caught on** in big way as shown by the increased sales.

contains a preposition↵ phrasal verb contains a preposition = **on**

. Prepositional phrases are discussed under phrases. Ending a statement with a preposition, e.g. '**this is the salesman I gave the money to**'

can offend some people. It is acceptable in informal English. It is a good idea to avoid this type of construction. In formal writing, it should be written as:

'**this is the salesman to whom I gave the money.**'

Conjunctions

Often a sentence is composed of two or more clauses which are joined together by one or more words. We also join words of equal status together by one or more words to form phrases. Words which we use to perform this function form their own word class called conjunctions. For instance:

. She is Sara **and** he is Simon. ⇐ compound sentence

clause a↵   ⇑   clause b↵

conjunction

. <u>That night was very cold,</u> **but** <u>there was no rain.</u>⇐ compound sentence

clause a↵ ⇑ clause b↵

conjunction

There is no need to insert commas between short clauses.

. <u>**Fast**</u> **and** <u>**accurate**</u> ⇐ phrase

adjective↵ adjective↵

. <u>Tea</u> **or** <u>coffee</u>

noun↵ noun↵

In the first two examples, conjunctions '**and**' and '**but**' join clauses within compound sentences. In the last two examples, conjunctions '**and**' and '**or**' link words of equal status, that is nouns, together.

Compound Sentences and phrases **See** ⇒ Phrases, Clauses and Sentences

. <u>Classes of conjunction</u>

We can classify conjunctions as:

> . **coordinating conjunctions or coordinators**

> . **subordinating conjunctions or subordinators**

. <u>Coordinating conjunctions or coordinators</u>

Coordinators are used to join two or more clauses of <u>**equal status**</u> in a compound sentence as illustrated above. Here are some more examples:

. <u>I went to my bank,</u> **and** <u>my wife did some shopping</u>.

clause 1↵ conjunction↵ clause 2↵

. <u>We were also on the motorway,</u> **but** <u>were not involved in that accident.</u>

clause 1↵ conjunction↵ clause 2↵

<u>There is no need to repeat the subject in clause 2 because both clauses have the same subject, that is **we**.</u>

. <u>My students are on a trip to London</u> **so** <u>I can mark their homework.</u>

clause 1↵ conjunction↵ clause 2↵

> **There are only a few most common coordinators:**
> **and, but, or, so, nor, yet**
> Coordinator 'nor' is the negative counterpart of 'or'.

. **Correlative coordinators** – Some coordinators function in pairs and are
called correlative coordinators. These are:

> **both...and, but...also, either...or, neither...nor, whether...or**

Correlative coordinators are very helpful in a variety of ways. For instance:
. to suggest alternative means of achieving something
. to place emphasis on some aspect of your statement
. to indicate a negative situation

Here are some examples to illustrate the advantages of using correlative coordinators:

. Sentences can be **either** simple **or** compound.

placing emphasis on alternative forms of sentences – implying that
what you are saying equally applies to both forms that are **simple** and
compound

. On receiving this news, we felt **both** a great joy **and** uneasiness.
emphasizing the emotions experienced↵

. **Neither** Adam **nor** Daniel was there.

expressing a negative situation

. <u>Subordinating conjunctions or subordinators</u>

Subordinators enable us to:
. link clauses of **unequal status** in complex sentences
. join sentences

. introduce subordinate clauses and

. show association between main and subordinate clauses

The following is a short list of some subordinators:

after, as long as, as soon as, assuming that, before, even if, except, in case, in order to, provided that, such, such as, till, unless, until, whether,...

Here are some examples of their application:

. We left home at 9 hours **before** the postman delivered the post.

main clause ↵   ⇑   subordinate clause↵

subordinator

indicating time

. Police found out **where** it was.

indicating place↵

. I am suffering from a stomach disorder **because** I ate too much.

indicating cause/reason↵

. We think it will be better **if** you negotiate.

predicting outcome/result ↵

. They sent us a reminder letter **so that** we can pay their money

result/outcome↵

. **As long as** you pay monthly instalments, your home is safe.

⇑

stating condition

. All of us will work tonight **in order that** information is ready for the

indicating purpose ↵   board meeting in the morning.

. Robert is efficient **while** John is inefficient.

indicating purpose↵

. All members were present **except** the chairperson who was ill.

indicating exception↵

. It was **rather** a difficult question for this group of students.
indicating opinion↵

. It looks **as though** they will not buy any more from us.
⇑
indicating comparison between now and future

. Our sales this years are higher **than** they were last year.
indicating comparison↵

These examples illustrate that conjunctions can help to express a wide range of meanings. Some subordinators such as **'in order that'** are listed in some quality dictionaries as idioms. In fact, it does not matter much what they are called. What is most important is that you know how to use these correctly.

. As words can be placed in more than one word class, some conjunctions can function as adverbs and prepositions. It all depends on the context in which these conjunctions are used. For instance:

. We have not supplied you goods **since** last December.
functioning as a preposition↵

In this example, **since** is linking 'last December' with the rest of the sentence.

. We have not supplied you goods **since** you bought a cooker from us.
⇑
subordinating conjunction linking two clause within this sentence

. John wrote to us about three months ago but we have not heard from him **since**.
⇑
functioning as an adverb – it is qualifying 'have not heard'

. In what specific way do conjunctions differ from prepositions and adverbs?

It is true to say that conjunctions are very helpful when you want to link parts of a sentence together. You have seen above that conjunctions do not add any information, like both prepositions and adverbs, which enhance the meaning of a statement by qualifying the relevant part to which they refer.

<u>Determiners and Interjections</u>

A small number of words form their own word class known as determiners. We use these words in front of a noun or a noun phrase. The obvious reason for calling them determiners is that they determine some specific qualities of a noun or noun phrase, e.g.

. **<u>The</u>** <u>Queen</u>.

determiner↵ noun↵

We can have a movie queen, a beauty queen, a carnival queen, etc. In the UK, 'The Queen' implies 'constitutional monarch'. Thus, the placing of a determiner '**the**' attaches this specific quality or importance to the noun 'queen'. It shows uniqueness – just one queen who is the constitutional monarch in the UK. Here is another example:

. **<u>The</u>** <u>United Nations Charter</u>. ⇐ noun phrase

determiner↵   noun phrase↵

There is only one United Nations Charter because there is only one United Nations in the entire world. The determiner emphasizes this uniqueness – attaches this specific quality to this noun phrase.

. <u>Kinds of Determiners</u>

Determiners are divided into two groups namely definite and indefinite determiners. These are listed in Table 17. In older grammar books, you may find these listed as adjectives. Here are some examples of each kind of determiner:

. <u>Definite article</u>

As shown in Table 17, '**the**' is the only definite article. The following examples illustrate its application in a wide range of contexts:

. <u>The</u> Palace Theatre is in London's West End.

referring to a unique ↵ - ⇒ 'Palace Theatre'

. This is my home. It is **the** house where I was born.

determining which noun is being referred to – attaching importance
to a noun ⟹ house
          . We were in France at **the** weekend.

     noun phrase referring to time ↵
          . He came from **the** Republic of Ireland.

when a country's name includes 'republic' or 'kingdom' the definite article
comes before it
          . We have a branch in **the** North as well.

when the name of a region is not preceded by an adjective, 'the' is used to
determine it
          . She lives in **the** Bahamas since last year.

when the name of a country is in the plural form, 'the' comes before it
          . In these days, vegetables are weighed by **the** kilograms.

the definite article comes before the noun indicating how something is
weighed or measured
     . She can bring with her **the** sewing machine given to her by grandmother.

          it is before a unique thing – unique to this family
. **The** managing director has retired today

'the' comes before a noun when the noun refers to a status

. **The** Duke of Edinburgh. ⟸ 'the' used here with the title

. Some domestic pets enjoy **the** music played on the radio.

'the' precedes an uncountable noun because 'music' refers to object
'the radio'.

The requirement is that '**the**' can precede an uncountable noun, if it refers to
an object or some specific thing or person. In the above example, '**music**' is

an uncountable singular noun that refers to 'the radio', which is an object.

The word radio can be both an uncountable and a countable noun. The definite article can precede the word radio but not always. For instance:

     . I wrote it for radio.

     . It was on radio and television.

     . It was on **the** radio last night.

         ⇑

     see the explanation for the last example

  . We met this publishing house at the Frankfurt Book Fair.

world's annual book trade exhibition centre↵ - largest book fair

  . The Central Bank of the European Union is in Frankfurt.
  . The Albert and Victoria Museum is worth visiting.

  . The Portrait Gallery is just behind the National Gallery.

These examples illustrate that the definite article precedes the names of museums, galleries, entertainment places, trade centres and similar organisations of public interest.

. **Indefinite articles**

There are only two indefinite articles '**a**' and '**an**' as shown in Table 17. The indefinite article '**an**' is placed in front of singular nouns that begin with a vowel (**a, e, i, o, u**), e.g.

     . The girl who is holding **an** umbrella is my daughter.
     . Could I have **an** envelope, please?

In the following examples, the definite article '**a**' precedes the noun:

     . It is **a** letter from a prospective client.

       ⇑   a = one

   before a singular noun in a noun phrase

     . Tonight is **a** very stormy night.

        ⇑   a = one

    before a noun phrase

. Mr Henderson is **a** lawyer.
⇑ a = one
it indicates someone's profession
. Miss Lyons is **a** member of our club.

These indefinite articles are discussed at length in another section of the book.
See ⇒ Troublesome Words and Phrases

• Kinds of determiners are listed in Table 17.

Kinds of determiners

Definite Determiner	Indefinite Determiners
definite article: the	**indefinite articles:** a, an
Possessive determiners: my, your, his, her, their, our, its <u>only seven words in this group</u> **note** possessive determiner 'its' is spelled without an apostrophe.	**indefinite determiners:** all, almost, another, any, both, each, either, enough, every, few, fewer, fewest, little, less, least, many, more, most, much, no, neither, other, several, some
Demonstrative determiners: this, that, these, those	**interrogative determiners:** what, which, whose

Numerals:
    cardinal: one, two, three,..
    Ordinal: first, second, third,...
    fraction: a quarter, two-thirds,
                    a tenth,...	

Table 17

. <u>Possessive determiners</u>

These determiners are used when you want to indicate possession or relation-ship. A possessive determiner qualifies a noun, which means it informs us to whom something belongs.

In the following examples possessive determiners are **<u>underlined</u>** because they are qualifying a noun which is also <u>underlined</u> :

> . <u>My mother</u> is a doctor.
> . Where is <u>your stock control file</u>?

. <u>Possessive determiners can precede an adjective or an intensifier, e.g.</u>

> . They have received <u>our</u> smallest parcel.
>   1⌐   2⌐   3⌐
> 1= possessive determiner   2 = superlative adjective   3= noun

This way, the possessive determiner is in front both 2 and 3.

. <u>If you want to emphasize that something belongs to a particular person or thing, you can place the adjective '**own**' after the possessive determiner, e.g.</u>
> . It was <u>her</u> own idea to travel by coach to Scotland.

. <u>Only one specific possessive determiner is used before a noun, e.g.</u>

> . I carried <u>my</u> suitcase to the rail station.
> . I carried my <u>the</u> suitcase to the rail station.

> incorrect use ⌐ - two determiners are not allowed.

<u>If you want to use the definite article, you can say:</u>

> . I carried <u>the</u> suitcase to the rail station.

This sentence does not mean the same as the previous sentence. <u>It does not indicate possession. Thus, you have to construct a sentence to convey your intended meaning.</u>

. <u>You must use the possessive determiner in accordance with the identification of the person or thing to whom something or someone relates, e.g.</u>

. You must operate <u>your own shop</u> to increase <u>your profit</u>.

. The project team met for <u>**its**</u> meeting in my office.

possessive determiner before the noun ↵ noun⟹ meeting

. Most colleges and **their** properties belong to the public.

. I am holding something in **my** right hand.

. <u>Possessive determiners are also used in titles, e.g.</u>

. **Her** Majesty the Queen   . **His** Excellency the French Ambassador

. **Demonstrative determiners**

There are only four such determiners. A demonstrative pronoun functions as a demonstrative determiner **only**, if it precedes the noun. In the following examples '**this**', '**these**', '**that**' and '**those**' are functioning as demonstrative determiners:

. <u>'**This**' is used for a singular person or thing that is near to you in place or space of time, e.g.</u>

. <u>This</u> ball is my property.

implying the ball is near to you (place) now(space of time)

precedes a singular noun ⟹ **ball**

. In <u>this</u> house my father was born.

. <u>The demonstrative determiner '**these**' relates to plural persons or things that are near to you physically or space of time, e.g.</u>

. <u>These</u> students are invited to take part in **this** debate.

indicating students are close (place) to you now(time)

- precedes a plural noun ⟹ **students**

. As soon as I have read **these** documents, I will telephone you.

. <u>Both '**this**' and '**these**' are also used to express time, e.g.</u>

. <u>This</u> year we will attend a national conference in Brighton

current year ↵ - precedes a singular noun

. **This day**, one year ago, I become a father.

In this example, '**this day**' refers to the current day and relates it to the past in terms of date.

. '**That**' and '**those**' refer to people or things which are not so close to you in terms of distance or space of time, or you can see them but they are far from you, e.g.

> . That _person is our new colleague.
> . That lady who is wearing a big hat is Princess Anne.
> . These days he takes life easy.

a period of time↵

> . How much is it for **that** round table?
> . Could you send me one of **those** fact sheets?

. Interrogative determiners:

To be interrogative determiners words '**what**', '**which**', and '**whose**' must precede a noun, e.g.

> . Whose house is this?

preceded a noun ↵ - noun ⇒house

> . Whose chair is broken?

preceded a noun ↵ - noun ⇒chair

> . Which European country has the largest land?

preceded a noun ↵ - noun ⇒European country

> . Which shop assistant served you?

preceded a noun ↵ - noun ⇒shop assistant

> . What time is it to come to work?

preceded a noun ↵ - noun ⇒ time

> . What colour is your favourite?

preceded a noun ↵ - noun ⇒colour - asking to specify a particular colour

. Indefinite determiners

There are some words that can function as indefinite determiners, if they modify/qualify a noun. Here are some examples:

. In this group **most** students work hard.

⇑

indefinite determiner modifying 'students'

. **Both** players are equally first class sportsmen.

⇑

indefinite determiner modifying noun ⇒ players

. **Many** people like listening to the radio for news.
. She does not like **any** ball sport.

In the last two examples, '**many**' and '**any**' are also functioning as indefinite determiners.

. Numeral determiners

These are exemplified under cardinal, ordinal and fractions below:

a)   These are cardinal numbers, e.g.

. There are **ten** passengers on this coach.

. Our company has **eight** delivery vans and **3** cars far sales staff.
. The total population of this town is **59,000** inhabitants.
. About **1,000,000** people watched the closing ceremony on

a million/one million ↵   all five national television channels.

In these examples, cardinal numbers are underlined. As you can see, these can be written in both words and numbers.

b)   Some ordinal numbers are exemplified below:

. Today is my grandson's **2nd** birthday.
. The **21st** century began five years ago.
. Who won the **first** prize tonight?

c)   The following examples show how to use fractions:

. It is about **three quarter** metres long.
. I was late **one hour and a** half.

'a' is essential here ↵

You can also express this as:

> . I was **one and a half hours** late.
>> 'hours' plural⤶
> . Our stock level is **one third of** its normal level. Order some more.
>> ⇑

'**of**' is essential in this noun phrase as the number is less than '**one**'

. Interjections (Exclamations !)

These are two very small word classes, which deserve discussion. These are interjections and particles. Interjections or exclamations form a minor word class. In fact, you can construct correct sentences without using a single interjection or exclamation. They are used to express something emphatically. In writing, the use of interjections is indicated by the use of an exclamation mark (**!**) at the end of a statement. In speech, interjection is shown by your intonation. Here are some interjections:

---

aha, alas, blast, bother, damn, good gracious, goodness me, gosh, oh, oh dear, ouch, really, what, wow, you're joking, ugh, yuck

---

Often interjections are used to show a reaction, e.g.

> . Johan was here a few minutes ago. **Oh** yes, how is he?
>> ⇑

reacting to information that you did not know before

. A noun, noun phrase or noun clause can function as an exclamation, e.g.

> . We went to see a play at the Royal Palace. **Quite a show**!
>> noun phrase acting as interjection⤶ indicating view
> . **What** a naive woman she is!
> . We have received our money. **Really!**
>> indicating surprise⤶

In formal writing, it is best to avoid the use of interjections shown in the above box. In informal English, you can use them.

. Particles

It is the smallest word class. A particle is used with a verb to form a multi-word verb or phrasal verb, e.g.

> . Our plan <u>took off</u>.

phrasal verb ↵ - and **off** ⟹ particle

> . Can you please **fill** my glass **up**?

Here:

> **fill up** ⟹ phrasal verb and **up** ⟹ particle

> . Please **hand** this knife **over** to me.

Here:

> **hand over** ⟹ phrasal verb and **over** ⟹ particle

> . She **fell off** her bicycle and hurt her knees.

Here:

> **fell off** ⟹ phrasal verb **and off** ⟹ particle

> . Suddenly our bus engine cut out.

Here:

> **cut out** ⟹ phrasal verb and **out** ⟹ particle

Words 'off', 'up', 'out' 'over', etc. belong to other word classes. When these words are used to form phrasal verbs then they are considered as particles. In fact, some writers do not discuss particles as a word class of their own.

Phrases, Clauses & Sentences

A phrase consists of a small number of words* and has a particular meaning. It can stand alone. It is usually a part of a clause or sentence. It is, therefore, smaller than a clause or sentence. It functions as a grammatical unit without a finite verb. For instance:

- . my youngest son   ⇐ standing alone- contains no finite verb
- . on last Monday   ⇐ standing alone - contains no finite verb
- . gorgeous day   ⇐ standing alone - contains no finite verb
- . in my car   ⇐ standing alone - contains no finite verb

---

* In a strict grammatical sense – a phrase may consist of one or more words. The word 'phrase' to many people means a small group of words.

. Types of phrases

Phrases can be identified as:
- . **noun phrase**   . **verb phrase**
- . **adverb phrase**   . **adjective phrase**
- . **prepositional phrase**

. How can you distinguish one type from the other types?

The most important aspect of the phrase structure is that a phrase has a:
>. **keyword** or **headword**

It gives the most important information. Its elimination from the phrase can change the structure and the intended meaning of the phrase. For this reason, the headword determines the type of a particular phrase. The headword may be a noun, pronoun, verb, adverb, adjective or preposition. The headword may be at the beginning or at the end of the phrase. Here are some examples:

. Noun phrases

The headword in a noun phrase is a noun (or pronoun). The headword may be preceded by a determiner. In addition, it can also be preceded by more than one modifier. In fact, a modifier can also come after the headword. For instance:

> . my **brother**

> headword/noun⏎ - phrase type ⟹ noun phrase

> . our **motherland**

> headword/noun⏎ - phrase type ⟹ noun phrase

. These are two simple noun phrases. In the following example, the pronoun 'you' stands alone as the headword. In a strict grammatical sense, it is also a noun phrase.

> . **you**

> pronoun on its own ⏎ - noun phrase

. **Usually noun phrases are incorporated into clauses and sentences, e.g.**

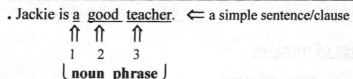

> . Jackie is a good teacher. ⟸ a simple sentence/clause
>   ⇑ ⇑ ⇑
>   1 2   3
>   ⎩ **noun phrase** ⎠

In this noun phrase:
1= determiner/ indefinite article - indicating one person
2 = adjective qualifying the noun (headword) teacher –giving additional
    information about the teacher – modifying/qualifying the noun – teacher
    good is a pre-modifier. A **premodifier** comes in front of the headword
3= headword = teacher

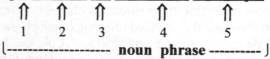

> . I am eating a delicious hot home-made chicken pie.
>   ⇑   ⇑   ⇑   ⇑   ⇑
>   1   2   3   4   5
>   ⎩----------------- **noun phrase** ----------⎠

It is further analysed as follows:

1= determiner/indefinite article   2= adjective - premodifier
3= adjective – premodifier   4= adjective – premodifier
5= headword noun

This example illustrates that there can be more than one premodifier. One should limit the use of premodifiers. Usually, up to three premodifiers do not make the phrase verbose.

. Sometimes the headword is **postmodified** that is the modifier comes after the headword, e.g.

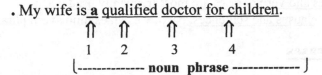

. My wife is <u>a</u> <u>qualified</u> <u>doctor</u> <u>for children</u>.

It is further analysed as follows:

1 = indefinite article   2= adjective   3 = headword = noun
4 = postmodifier -comes after the headword

Postmodifers are more complex than premodifiers. The reason is that the postmodfier may be another phrase. In this example:

'for children' is a prepositional phrase that is functioning as a postmodifier.

. In the following example, the headword is also postmodified by a prepositional phrase:

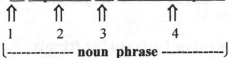

. She drives <u>an</u> <u>expensive</u> <u>car</u> <u>all over the place</u>.

In this example:

1 = indefinite article   2= adjective   3 = headword = noun
4 = postmodifier -comes after the headword - prepositional phrase

. It is possible that a noun phrase is followed by another noun phrase. If so, the purpose of the second noun phrase is to give some explanatory information about the headword, e.g.

. <u>Jawaharlal Nehru,</u> <u>the father of Indira Gandhi</u>, was also a politician.

first noun phrase   second noun phrase

. The City of London, the financial district of London, has many banks.
⇑   ⇑
    first noun phrase   second noun phrase

In such constructions, the second noun phrase is known as '**an apposition**' to the first phrase.

. Noun phrases and verb phrases are most frequently used when constructing clauses and sentences. Next, we can examine verb phrases.

. Verb phrases

A simple verb phrase has a lexical verb as its headword. This lexical verb may be a multi-word. Auxiliary verbs are **not** included in lexical verbs. A complex verb phrase has a lexical verb as its headword and one or more auxiliary verbs. Here are some examples:

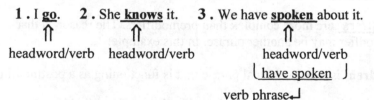

1 . I **go**.   **2** . She **knows** it.   **3** . We have **spoken** about it.
⇑   ⇑   ⇑
headword/verb   headword/verb   headword/verb
                                       ⌊ have spoken ⌋

                           verb phrase⌋

. In examples 1-2, headwords are in the base form of the verb '**go**' and present '**– s**' form of the verb '**know**' respectively. In example 3, the verb phrase consists of the auxiliary verb '**have**' plus the past participle form of the irregular verb '**speak**'.

  . She **has** **been** **writing** letters to her friends.
    ⇑ ⇑   ⇑
    1 2   3
    ⌊ verb phrase ⌋

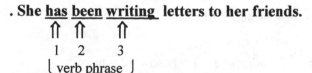

1= present form of the primary auxiliary ' have
2 = past participle for of the primary auxiliary verb 'be'
3 = participle '-ing' form of the finite verb 'write*

Verb phrases are central to the construction of clauses and sentences. The other important feature of verb phrases is **tense**. Tenses are discussed under their own section.

* See ⟹ sentences See ⟹ tenses

. Adverb phrases

An adverb phrase has an adverb as its headword. It can only be the headword
alone or a small group of words that has an adverb as its headword and some
other elements, e.g.
> . She writes <u>slowly</u>.

> > adverb↵ - headword = slowly
> . Your letter does not give arrival time <u>clearly</u>.

> > > adverb phrase↵ - headword = clearly
> . We discussed this matter <u>after the contract</u> was signed.

> > > adverb phrase↵ – headword = after = adverb
> . We used to exchange letters <u>quite regularly</u> for some years.

> > 1↵   2↵

In this example: 1 = adverb premodifying the headword 'regularly'
> > > > it is intensifying the meaning of the adverb 'regularly'
> > > 2= headword = adverb = regularly

Another example:
> . We arrived **promptly** **at 14 hours**.

> > 1↵   2↵

> 1= headword = adverb
> 2 = prepositional phrase which is postmodifying the headword.
> > adding further information

. Adjective phrases

Adjective phrases are similar to adverb phrases. Like adverb phrases, adjective phrases can be modified. An adjective phrase has an adjective as its
headword, e.g.
> > . Janet is <u>thin</u>.

> adjective/headword↵ - adjective phrase standing alone

> > . Keith is <u>very quick</u>.

> > > 1↵ 2↵
> > > ⌊adjective phrase⌋

1= adverb is intensifying the meaning of the headword
2= headword = quick = adjective

. After the job interview, he felt <u>so</u> <u>dejected</u>.

                 1⤶   2⤶

1= adverb modifying the headword

2= adjective = head word

           . Karin is <u>intelligent</u> <u>enough</u> for this job.

                  1⤶   2⤶

         1= adjective = headword

         2. adverb – postmodifying the headword ⟹ intelligent

. **Prepositional phrases**

Until now you have learnt that the headword can stand alone as a phrase. This is not the case as far as prepositional phrases are concerned. In this respect, prepositional phrases differ from other types of phrases. The structure of a prepositional phrase consists of the headword that is a preposition together with the prepositional complement, which is ,often, a noun phrase. This can be simplified as:

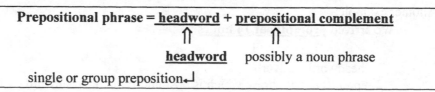

Here are some examples:

          . We have been communicating **through** **letters**.

                          1⤶   2⤶

                          ⌊ prepositional ⌋
                             phrase

In this example: 1 = headword ⟹ preposition

               2 = noun phrase⟹ prepositional complement

   . We are here in Berlin **because of** <u>your</u> <u>wedding celebrations tomorrow.</u>

                   1⤶   2⤶

                   ⌊----- ------- **prepositional phrase** --------------⌋

1= headword = group preposition

2= prepositional complement ⟹postmodifying the headword

___

- I only met him <u>during</u> <u>my stay</u> <u>in London</u>.

  1⌐   2⌐   3⌐

  1= headword ⟹ preposition
  2= noun phrase postmodifying the headword

  3 = another prepositional phrase with headword ⟹ **in**

. **Embedded phrases**

Phrases can be embedded within each other, e.g.

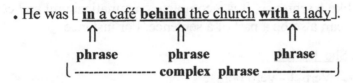

In this example, the complex phrase consists of three main phrases. We can analyse this complex phrase into smaller phrases by means of the **recursion process** in order to show that phrases are embedded within each other. In the following analysis, the headword in each phrase is **highlighted**:

⌐ **in** a café behind the church with a lady⌐ ⟹ prepositional phrase
⌐ a **café** behind the church with a lady⌐ ⟹ noun phrase
⌐ **behind** the church with a lady⌐ ⟹ prepositional phrase
⌐ the **church** with a lady⌐ ⟹ noun phrase
⌐ **with** a lady⌐ ⟹ prepositional phrase
⌐ a **lady**⌐ ⟹ noun phrase

The above analysis demonstrates that phrases are embedded within each other in such a manner that the highest level phrase contains all other phrases. The lowest level phrase is embedded within the next level and the pattern is repeated until all the phrases are embedded in the highest level phrase. This process is known as the recursion process.

. **Noun Phrases in apposition**

If two noun phrases come one after the other and both refer to the same person or thing, then phrases are in apposition. For instance:

- Mr. Putin, the president of the Federation of Russia, is a Karate expert.

This sentence has two adjacent phrases:

. Mr. Putin $\Rightarrow$ noun phrase 1

. the president of the Federation of Russia $\Rightarrow$ noun phrase 2

. We saw <u>Buckingham Palace in London,</u> <u>the London office of</u>
<u>the Queen.</u>

In both examples, phrases are in apposition.

. <u>Clauses</u>

A group of some words that include a subject and a verb is a clause. A clause is just like a sentence. It is a complete grammatical unit and can stand alone. It can also be a part of a sentence. For instance:

(1) . She <u>has left</u>.

subject⌐ Verb⌐ - verb phrase

(2) . <u>I</u> <u>write</u> <u>this note</u>.

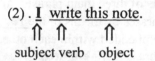

subject verb   object

. <u>Clause elements</u>

Clauses are constructed by combining some or all of the following five clause elements:

. Subject $\Rightarrow$ S   . Verb $\Rightarrow$ V   . Object $\Rightarrow$ O

. Complement $\Rightarrow$ C   . Adverbial $\Rightarrow$ A

As shown by the above two examples <u>subject</u> (S) and <u>verb</u> (V)elements are essential for a construction to be a clause.

. <u>Subject element (S)</u>

The subject element comes before the verb element, e.g.

. <u>Cherie</u> <u>loves</u> <u>flowers</u>.

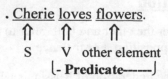

S   V   other element

⌐- **Predicate**------⌐

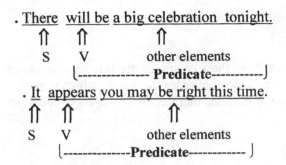

These examples illustrate:

. subject occurs in the subject position before the **verb**
. sometimes in the subject position an **empty or dummy subject**
  is placed. An empty subject is not related to any specific person or
  thing
. '**there**' and '**it**' are dummy or empty subjects as shown in the last
  two examples
. it is possible to rewrite the sentence without the empty subject, e.g.

   . Tonight there will be a big celebration = There will be a big
                                                   celebration tonight.

. **When do you use a dummy subject?**

   . If a phrase begins with '**a**' or '**an**' (indefinite articles), usually, it does
     not start a sentence. In such cases, the dummy subject begins the
     sentence.
   . When the verb '**be**' is followed by '**a**', '**an**' or '**some**', the dummy
     subject begins the sentence.

. **Verb element (S)**

The verb element is the main focus of a clause. Without it, an action or a
state cannot be expressed by the clause, e.g.

         . She <u>feels</u> her love for her newly born baby.
      verb element⏎
            . We <u>were discussing</u> this matter for several hours.
         verb element⏎

. There <u>will be</u> a national strike against the government.

verb element↵

If you eliminate verb elements from these examples, the intended meanings will not be expressed at all. The subject initiates the theme, which is expressed in terms of the action or the state that the writer wishes to communicate.

. <u>Object element (O)</u>

The object element comes after the verb element, e.g.

. I like <u>milk</u>.

object ↵ - like ⟹ transitive verb

. I will tell <u>you all.</u>

object ↵ - tell ⟹ transitive verb

Objects are noun phrases. These example demonstrate that a transitive verb takes an object element.

. <u>A clause can have both direct and indirect objects, e.g.</u>

. I presented [to] <u>Cherie</u> **some flowers**.

indirect object ↵direct object↵

In this example, the **primary effect** of the verb presented [to] is on 'some flowers'. For this reason, it is the **direct object**. There is no need to use 'to' after the verb 'presented'. This is why 'to' is enclosed within [ ].

Since some flowers were presented to Cherie, the **secondary effect** of the verb 'presented' is on Cherie. For this reason, Cherie is the **indirect object**.

. We borrowed **some money** for <u>our honeymoon</u>.

direct object ↵ indirect object↵

Indirect object is preceded by **for** ⟹ preposition

. <u>Sometimes a clause functions as an object, e.g.</u>

. We assure you our <u>representative will meet you at the airport</u>.

a clause functioning as an object ↵

. <u>Complement element (C)</u>

A complement may be a word or a group of words. It comes after a copular verb or a transitive verb that takes an object and object complement, e.g.

. He **seems** a <u>rich businessman</u>.

linking verb⤶   ⇑

         subject complement

A complement that comes after a linking verb is known as the **subject complement.** In fact, this subject complement is a noun phrase. In other words, in this case, the noun phrase is acting as the subject complement.

. Hanna **looked** <u>disappointed</u>.

linking verb⤶   ⇑

       subject complement

The subject element expresses the subject's attribute(s) as indicated above. In this example, the subject complement is an adjective phrase. <u>The subject complement is also known as the **subject predicative.**</u>

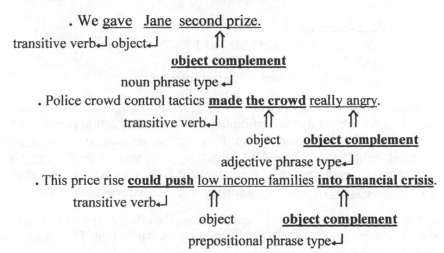

. We <u>gave</u>   <u>Jane</u>   <u>second prize</u>.

transitive verb⤶ object⤶   ⇑

            object complement

      noun phrase type ⤶

. Police crowd control tactics **made** **the crowd** <u>really angry</u>.

         transitive verb⤶   ⇑   ⇑

               object   **object complement**

           adjective phrase type⤶

. This price rise **could push** <u>low income families</u> **into financial crisis**.

       transitive verb⤶   ⇑   ⇑

           object   **object complement**

       prepositional phrase type⤶

The object complement describes the object as shown above. <u>The object complement is also called the object predicative.</u>

. **Adverbial element (A)**

The adverbial element is either an adverb phrase or a prepositional phrase. A clause can also function as adverbial. The adverbial element can occur any-where in a clause, e.g.

. Andréa speaks English <u>very fluently</u>.

adverb phrase functioning like an adverbial↵

. Our client will not arrive <u>before 11 hours</u>.

prepositional phrase functioning like an adverbial↵

. He left school <u>at the age of 16</u>.

⇑

prepositional phrase functioning like an adverbial

As illustrated above, the adverbial element functions like an adverb. For this reason it is known by this name.

. Active voice

When the subject is the person or thing that is carrying out an action, which is indicated by the verb and the object is affected by the action, then the grammatical structure is known as the active clause or the active voice.
For instance:

   . <u>**My employers**</u> <u>appreciate</u> my efficiency.
   . <u>**Thousands of people**</u> <u>visit</u> this park everyday.
   . <u>**My wife**</u> <u>was driving</u> our car.
   . <u>**His family**</u> <u>saw</u> him this afternoon.

In these examples, the subject (or the agent) is shown in **bold style**. In each case, it is the subject that is performing the action. The action is indicated by the underlined verb or verb group. Furthermore, in each example, <u>it is the object element that is **affected** by the action of the verb or verb group. Since the performer of the action is the subject, it is also known as the **agent**. A verb also describes a state or condition</u>, e.g.   . He loves his family.

In this case, the subject /agent is experiencing the effect of the verb 'loves' and the object 'family' is affected by the love shown by him. Therefore, it is also an active voice or active clause.

. Passive voice

On the other hand, when the subject is the person or thing that is affected by the action or the state (such as hunger) it is the passive voice. The clause that has a verb or verb group that creates the passive voice is called the passive clause. Passive voice is just the opposite of the active voice. These are exemplified below:

. My efficiency is appreciated by **my employers**.
. This park is visited, everyday, by **thousands of people**.
. Our car has been driven by **my wife**.
. He was seen by **his family this afternoon**.
. His family is loved by **him**.

The active voice or active clause is considered as **the primary structure**.
The passive voice or clause is transformed from the primary voice. This can be seen by comparing the above active and passive clauses. It is not always possible to make this transformation as not all transitive verbs can be converted to the passive form.

The passive voice is more formal than the active voice. However, in speech, usually it is the active voice that is more frequently used. The passive voice is useful when you do not know the agent or wish to avoid mentioning it.

. Finite clauses

In a finite clause, the verb is inflected for tense in accordance with the person, e.g.

> . Amanda **works** for Boyes.

finite verb **work** inflected in accordance with the person(Amanda) and **simple present tense**

> . Rachel **has been working** for the Home Office since 2000.

finite verb **work** is inflected in accordance with the person (Rachel) and **present perfect continuous tense**

. Non-finite clauses

In a non-finite clause, the verb is **not** marked for tense. It can be a part of a bigger or higher level clause which is marked for tense. If you isolate the non-finite clause from the higher level clause, the non-finite clause does not appear to be grammatically correct or complete. Here are some examples:

> . I was in Paris **to attend** a conference.

non-finite clause with to-infinitive - without subject

. <u>**Conference ended**</u> we went for a drink in the same hotel

⇑

non-finite clause - with subject

. My wife developed the software <u>**set up the system**</u>

⇑

non-finite clause - without subject

In this example, the elements of the non-finite clause are:

. subject ⇒ missing   . verb ⇒set up   . object ⇒ system

In practice, non of these finite clauses can stand alone. However, when a non-finite clause is within a higher level clause without the subject, the subject has to be guessed. On the contrary, the finite clause always has a subject element.

.**Classification of clauses**

Basically, clauses are classified as <u>**main**</u> and <u>**subordinate**</u> clauses.

. I have made it.
. We have written to each other last month.
. She likes red roses very much.

<u>**These are main clauses**</u> as each clause does not require any other information to be grammatically complete. Without any further information, they make syntactical sense. Main clauses are also known as <u>**independent clauses**</u> because they do not need any other information to be meaningful.

. <u>Subordinate clauses</u>

A subordinate clause cannot stand alone and must be used with a main clause. When a statement is complex, we construct a sentence in such a way that it has <u>**one main clause**</u> that expresses the main meaning and add one or more clauses that refer to <u>**some subordinate meanings**</u>. Clauses that support the main clause by means of adding subordinate meanings to the overall meaning of a statement are <u>**subordinate**</u> or <u>**dependent clauses**</u>. Here are some examples:

. <u>You must attend this function</u> <u>because</u> <u>it is very important for us</u>.

⇑   ⇑   ⇑

main clause   subordinating conjunction   subordinate clause

. They were burgled <u>while they were asleep</u>.
main clause↵   ⇑
                    subordinate beginning with 'while' conjunction

. <u>Classification of subordinate clauses</u>

> . **noun or nominal clauses**
> . **relative clauses**
> . **adverbial clauses**
> . **comparative clauses**

You may find some other classifications of clauses in some other books.

. <u>Noun or nominal clauses</u>

A noun clause is a group of words containing a finite verb and acts as
subject, object or complement, e.g.

. <u>We think</u> <u>that you will accept this offer</u>.
main clause↵   noun clause ↵
. I am pleased **that you will come**.
                    noun clause ↵
. We understand **that they were engaged to each other**.
noun clause acting as the object of the sentence↵

A noun clause does not always begin with **that, if, whether**, it can begin with
another conjunction or a question word. It is also called a nominal group.

. **Whether I can participate in this event** depends on my wife's health.
        ⇑
noun clause functioning as the **subject** of the sentence
. **That you won the race** was the best news for me.
        ⇑
clause functioning as the **subject** of the sentence

. When **'that'** starts the clause, it must do so even if it begins the sentence.
It is worth remembering that **'if'** cannot start a noun clause when it is
functioning as the subject of the sentence.

. <u>Relative clauses</u>

When a clause begins with any of the relative pronouns and refers to an earlier noun, pronoun or a noun phrase then it is a relative clause, e.g.

. <u>**The gentleman who**</u> is wearing a blue smart suit.

     ⇑   ⇑   ⇑

   noun phrase   relative pronoun   relative clause modifying
                                 the noun phrase

This clause is the **identifying clause** because it is pointing out which gentleman is meant. It is qualifying the noun phrase – **the gentleman**.

. Identifying clauses do not have commas before they begin with a relative pronoun.

   . The property **that** I inherited two years ago.

noun phrase↲   ⇑   ⇑

          relative pronoun   relative clause
                             identifying property

. Some relative clauses are **classifying clauses** because they indicate what kind of noun or noun phrase is meant. Like the identifying clauses, classifying clauses do not have commas before they begin with a relative pronoun.

   . He is **the best person whom** you can rely on.

   noun phrase↲   ⇑   ⇑

               relative pronoun relative clause

This classifying clause indicates what kind of person is meant.

   . I want to have **a list of customers** who do not pay on time.

            noun phrase↲   ⇑

                       relative clause /classifying clause

. Some relative clauses act as **adding** and **connective clauses**. Adding clauses give extra information about the noun /noun phrase. On the other hand, **connective clauses** inform us about something that has happened. **Adding and connective clauses** have commas, e.g.

. The building, **which is next to the white tower**, is our property.

                     ⇑ - commas before and after it

   adding clause giving additional information about the building

. She wore <u>a red dress,</u> **which** <u>her husband sent her from Paris</u>.

⇑

adding clause giving additional information about a red dress – noun phrase
You can leave out the adding clause and the sentence still makes sense.

<u>You can leave out the adding clause and the sentence still makes sense.</u>

. We asked the speaker, **who gave a long answer.**

             connective clause⤶

. We wrote to our representative, **who has not yet replied to us**.

             connective clause⤶

. <u>Can you leave out the relative pronoun in a relative clause?</u>

Yes. You can do so in informal English, providing the relative pronoun is not
the subject of the clause.

. <u>Comparative clauses</u>

Comparative clauses enable us to express comparison by using either a
subordinating conjunction **'than'** or correlative subordinators **'as---as'**.
The following examples demonstrate how to construct comparative clauses:

. <u>China's economy is growing much faster</u> **than some experts predicted**.

    main clause⤶   comparative clause begins with a subordinator⤶

. <u>She is far more knowledgeable about this subject</u> **than I had expected.**

    main clause⤶   comparative clause begins with a subordinator⤶

. I do not complaint about bad roads **as** <u>often</u> **as** other people do.

. He works **as** <u>efficiently</u> **as** some other members of staff work.

. <u>Adverbial clauses</u>

An adverbial clause in a complex sentence functions in the same way as an
adverb in a simple sentence. It modifies the main clause. An adverbial clause
is joined to the main clause by a conjunction. It can be placed at the beginning, in the middle or at the end of a sentence. It is used to express all kinds
of real-life situations. Here are some examples:

. We travelled to Japan **where we saw many amazing things**.

      adverbial clause of place ⤶- referring to place

. I was in Sweden **when I was about 24 years of age**.

    adverbial clause of time ↵ - referring to time

The adverbial clause refers to the way something is done or someone behaves or does something. In this example, we are concerned about the way he was walking.

. You must organise your spare time **in the way that is best for you**.

      adverbial clause of manner↵ - referring to doing something

. You can write to us **if you have the time to do so**

adverbial clause of condition ↵ - stating a condition

. He sent us this newspaper article **because it is about our area.**

    adverbial clause of reason ↵ - stating a reason

. **If you cannot afford to buy this large house**, you can buy a smaller one.

    adverbial clause of condition ↵

A comma is usually inserted at the end of an adverbial clause when it comes first as shown by the last two examples.

. Sentences

A sentence consists of a group of words, which are put together in accordance with some rules of grammar. It can be made of only a subject and a verb or extended by an object and object complement. It can be simple, complex or compound. It can express positive or negative meanings. Its structure can be declarative, interrogative, imperative or exclamative. If you compare it with other grammatical units namely a phrase or a clause, the sentence is the largest unit. In fact, sentences include both phrases and clauses. A sentence can be active or passive.

. Sentence construction

  . I go. . She **dances**.   . We go.   . They play.

            ⇑   ⇑ ⇑

    verb inflected   S   V

These are **simple sentences**. Each sentence has a subject(s) and a verb (v). In fact, these sentences can be considered as clauses. A simple sentence has at least one clause.

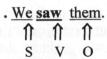

. We **saw** them.

⇑   ⇑   ⇑

S   V   O

This is also a simple sentence because it has only one clause with a finite verb 'saw' but it is extended in order to include 'object element'. Indeed, it is also a finite clause. The next two sentences are also simple but include both subject and object complements:

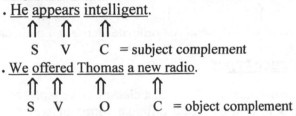

. He appears intelligent.

⇑   ⇑   ⇑

S   V   C   = subject complement

. We offered Thomas a new radio.

⇑ ⇑   ⇑   ⇑

S   V   O   C   = object complement

. As illustrated above, a simple sentence has only one verb or verb element.

. **Compound and complex sentences**

If we wish to put together two or more clauses in the form of a sentence, we can do so by creating either a compound or complex sentence. This is illustrated now.

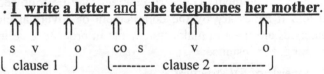

. **I write a letter** and **she telephones her mother**.

⇑ ⇑   ⇑   ⇑ ⇑   ⇑   ⇑

s   v   o   co   s   v   o

⌊ clause 1 ⌋   ⌊--------- clause 2 -----------⌋

In this sentence: co = coordinating conjunction or coordinator, joining two clauses of **grammatically equal status** to form **a compound sentence**

By equal status, it means two **main SVO clauses** as demonstrated above.
The coordinating conjunction/coordinator is essential and it must be placed between two main clauses. Clauses can change place without altering the structure and meaning of a compound sentence, e.g.

. She telephones her mother and I write a letter.

. It is possible to include more than two main clauses in a compound sentence. This can be achieved by using '**and**' and '**or**' coordinators between clauses, e.g.

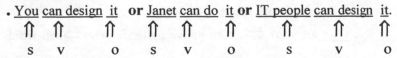

. You can design it   or Janet can do it **or** IT people can design it.

⇑   ⇑   ⇑   ⇑   ⇑   ⇑   ⇑   ⇑

S   V   O   S   V   O   S   V   O

. In contrast to the compound sentence, the **complex sentence** contains at least two or more clauses of **unequal grammatical status**. One clause is a main clause and one or more clauses are subordinate clauses, e.g.

> . **We were in the meeting when** someone knocked on the door.
>
> main clause⌐   conjunction⌐   subordinate clause⌐
>
> . **As soon as** we entered the room, **our competitors left the room**.

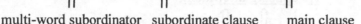

multi-word subordinator   subordinate clause   main clause

. Sentence types

The above discussion shows that clauses make sentences. The different combinations of clauses create different forms of sentences. Furthermore, the structures of clauses lead to declarative, interrogative, imperative and exclamative sentence types.

. Declarative sentences

These are by far the most common sentences. In such sentences, the subject is followed by the verb element. The verb element may be followed by an object element and if necessary by the complement or adverbial elements. Declarative sentences are used to make statements in order to give information about something. For instance:

. They eat. ⇐ consists of SV structure

. They eat junk food. ⇐ consists of SVO

. They eat junk food in a well-known restaurant. ⇐ consists of SVOA

. Interrogative sentences

Interrogative sentences generate answers in the form of yes/no or some specific information. These are questions. When the answer should be given by **'yes'** or **'no'**, the question is called **yes/no question**, otherwise, the question is **wh-question** . A **wh-question** begins with a **wh-word** such as what. This is demonstrated below:

> . We are students. ⇐ declarative sentence
>
> . **Who** are you? ⇐ interrogative sentence **who** ⇒ wh-word

(A) . She is working for the BBC in London. ⇐ declarative sentence

(B) . Is she working for the BBC in London? ⇐ interrogative sentence

Interrogative sentences can be formed by the process of **inversion** that involves changing the word order in a declarative sentence. The inversion process is applied to example(A) by changing the word order in such a way that the subject and the verb have changed their respective places. The example (B) is the result of inversion. Here is another example of inversion:

. They **wrote** to us some months ago. ⇐ declarative sentence

In order to convert this statement into an interrogative sentence, place the simple past form of the auxiliary verb '**do**' in the subject position. It is '**did**'. Also change the past participle verb form '**wrote**' to its base form '**write**', e.g.

. **Did** they write to us some months ago?

There are only the following nine wh-question words

what, who, whom, which, whose, where, when, why, how

. **You can also use negative words in interrogative sentences**.
  For instance:

. Have you told her **never** to jilt him?

. Why are **fewer** students in this class?

. Imperative sentences

The imperative sentence is constructed with the base form of the verb. It refers to the second person either singular or plural. The imperative type of sentence is often used for giving advice, warnings, instructions, directions, invitations, good wishes, et. For instance:

. Go away.   ⇐ order/ impolite manner

. Come in.   ⇐ permission

. Do come in.   ⇐ permission rather emphatic

. Get out quickly.   ⇐ advice/instruction/order

. Don't cry, please.   ⇐ advice/polite request

When someone says, **'come in'** it means **'you should come in'**. It is a form of giving a permission to enter. To many people, the imperative form can be rather impolite. It can be made less discourteous by giving orders in some other ways, e.g. **Would you please come in?**

This statement is rather polite but it is still in the form of an order.

. Exclamative sentences

When you want to express feelings and desires such as joy, sorrow, anger, surprise, etc. use exclamative sentences. In writing emphasis is indicated by the exclamation mark '**!**' Often they are constructed by using '**how**' and '**what**' wh-question words. For instance:
> . How lucky my brother was!   . How pleasing the news is!

. A phrase or a clause can be used as an exclamative sentence, e.g.

> . Lovely!   . Excellent performance!   . Oh no!
> . Goodness gracious!   . Aren't you happy now!

. Positive and negative sentences

The purpose of a positive sentence is to express positive meaning. The negative sentence shows negative sense. A positive sentence can be converted to a negative sentence and vice versa. Here are some examples:
> . He is a well-known gentleman in this area.⇐ positive sentence

> . He is **not** a well-known gentleman in this area.⇐ negative sentence

> . I prefer written communication. ⇐ positive sentence

. In this positive sentence, the verb '**prefer**' is in its base form because the sentence expresses the simple present tense. In such cases, the negative sentence is formed by adding to the positive sentence, in accordance with the subject and the tense of the sentence, a **dummy auxiliary verb** and '**not**'. Furthermore, the verb form must be changed accordingly so that the negative and positives sentences have the same tense. For instance:

> . I **do not** prefer written communication. ⇐ negative sentence

. Negative words such as '**never**', '**nothing**', '**nowhere**', '**no longer**', etc. can be inserted into the correct position in a sentence to make it negative, e.g. The most wanted file is **no longer** available.

Tenses

A tense is the verb form which indicates the time of an action or time of a state. The base form of the verb is inflected in such a way that it can be used to indicate the time of an action or the time of a state expressed by the verb. This can be achieved correctly when the **verb form**, **person** and **number** of the **subject** are in agreement. For instance:

. I wish.   . We go.   . You run.   . He/She loves.

state verb ⏎ action verb ⏎   action verb⏎ verb inflected ⏎ - state verb

A state implies something staying the same. In these examples, both action and state verbs indicate 'action' and 'state' at the present time (**now**) and thus the tense of these sentences is called the **simple present tense**. The verb inflection takes place only when the subject is 'third person singular'.

. Present progressive/continuous tense

You know well that events happen continuously at the present time. The present progressive indicates that the action or state is at the present time and it is continuous, e.g. I am writing it now. It is constructed as:

present progressive/continuous tense = present form of 'be' +
                                                     participle form of the verb '-ing'

. Simple past tense

The past tense describes an action or a state that has already happened at a particular time (**then**) as opposed to the simple present tense that relates to something which happens at the present time (**now**).The simple past tense is constructed by using the past participle form of the verb. The past participle verb form is the inflected verb form. For instance: She was happy.

It is constructed as:

past tense = past participle form of the verb

> ### Remember
>
> . the person and the number dictate the verb form
> . the time of the action is indicated by the inflected form of the verb

. Past progressive/continuous tense

It expresses some event happening continuously in the past, e.g.
> . I **was running** fast to catch my flight to nowhere.

It is constructed as:

> past progressive/continuous tense = past form of 'be' +
> participle form of the verb '-ing'

. Simple future tense

In our day-to-day life, we talk about some action or state that will happen after the present time. When we are looking ahead of the present time, we are looking into the future time. This is expressed by the simple future tense, e.g.
> . **I will visit you.** It is constructed as

> future tense = auxiliary will or shall + base/bare infinitive verb

> ### The present-day use of shall and will
>
> . with the first person subject use $\Rightarrow$ **shall or will**
>
> . with all other subjects use $\Rightarrow$ **will**

. Future progressive/continuous tense

It relates to an action or a state that will continue over a period of time in the future, e.g. . **I will be working in Birmingham.** It is constructed as:

> future progressive/continuous tense = shall/will 'be' + participle form
> of the verb '-ing'

. <u>Perfect or present perfect tense</u>

It expresses an action or a state that is completed in the near past up to the present time. You can think of the difference between the simple past and the present perfect tenses in terms of near past and past. When we say '**past**', we mean some time ago. It does not usually mean the past time that just has elapsed. For instance:

. I <u>left</u> London. ⇐ simple past tense
⇑

it means action of the verb was completed some time ago.

. I <u>**have left**</u> London. ⇐ present perfect tense
⇑

it means action of the verb was completed in the near past up to the present time – it can include even today. It is constructed as:

present perfect tense= present of auxiliary verb' have' + past participle
form of the verb

. <u>Present perfect progressive tense</u>

The present perfect progressive expresses an action or a state over a period of time in the past and is continuing up-to the present time, e.g.
. We **have been waiting** to hear from you since last month.
It is constructed as:

present perfect progressive tense= present of auxiliary verb' have'
+ 'been' + participle form '-ing'
of the verb

. <u>Past perfect tense</u>

The past perfect expresses the completion of an action or a state in the past time but a long time ago. It implies not near past but past that elapsed long ago, e.g.

. **I had lived in Lancashire in 1960's.** It is constructed as:

past perfect tense= past of auxiliary verb' have' + past participle
form of the verb

. Past perfect progressive tense

The past perfect progressive expresses the continuation of an action or a state in the past time but a long time ago, e.g.
                    . We **had been dancing** all night on that occasion.
It is constructed as:

---
past perfect progressive tense= past of auxiliary verb' have' + 'been'
                              + participle form '– ing' of the verb

---

. Future perfect tense

The future perfect tense expresses an action or a state that will be completed at a specific time in the future. The difference between the simple future and the future perfect is that the simple future refers to some events to happen in the future. On the other hand, the future perfect expresses the happening of something in the future and its completion at a specific point in time in the future. For instance:
              . They **will have carried** out their investigation by next June.

It is constructed as:

---
future perfect tense= will/shall +have+ past participle of the verb

---

. Future perfect progressive tense

The future perfect progressive is the progressive form of the future perfect tense but it shows continuity in the future, e.g.
. By next month, we will have been living in this town for twenty years.

It is constructed as:

---
future perfect progressive tense= will/shall + have+ been + participle
                              '-ing' form of the verb

. Future in the past tense

It is rather a difficult idea to grasp. If you imagine yourself in the past time and thinking in the past time about some action or state to happen in the future, you are referring to one of the following four types of future in the past tenses:

- I <u>should/would have</u> helped you. ⇐**simple future in the past**

contemplating in the past about the future action

It is constructed as:

> future in the tense= should/would + have+ past participle form
> of the verb

- I should/would be helping you. ⇐ **future progressive in the past**

It is constructed as:

> future progressive in the tense= should/would +be+
> participle 'ing' form of the verb

- I should/would have helped you. ⇐ **future perfect in the past**

It is constructed as:

> future perfect in the tense= should/would + have + past participle
> form of the verb

- I should/would have been helping you. ⇐ **future perfect**
> **progressive in the past**

It is constructed as:

> future perfect progressive in the tense= should/would + have + been +
> participle 'ing' form of the verb

A summary of tenses (active voice)

Present Simple	Past Simple	Future Simple	Simple future in the Past
I talk	I talked	I shall/will talk	I should/would talk
Present Progressive	**Past Progressive**	**Future Progressive**	**Future Progressive in the Past**
I am talking	I was talking	I shall/will be talking	I should/would be talking
Present Perfect	**Past Perfect**	**Future Perfect**	**Future Perfect in the Past**
I have talked	I had talked	I shall/will have talked	I should/would have talked
Present Perfect Progressive	**Past Perfect Progressive**	**Future Perfect Progressive**	**Future Perfect Progressive in the Past**
I have been talking	I had been talking	I shall/will have been talking	I should/would have been talking

Table 18

When we make a statement about an action or state that exists now, in the past or will happen in the future, we are referring to a point in time. This specific idea of point in time is at the heart of tenses. Tenses enable us to express an extensive range of astonishing meanings in both active and passive voices.

Part 2
Punctuation

The purpose of punctuation is to help the reader to pause in the right places. There are some rules and corresponding punctuation marks. The misuse of punctuation rules and marks or the absence of punctuation can lead to misunderstanding and ambiguity. If you can learn the following marks together with their rules, you should be able to punctuate from the reader's point of view.

. <u>Apostrophe</u>

An apostrophe has the following two main functions:

. to indicate possession or genitive case $\Rightarrow$ **Possessive Apostrophe**
. to mark contractions or show contractions or omissions of letters or

syllables in the spelling of some words $\Rightarrow$**Contraction Apostrophe**

Each of these functions is exemplified below:

1. <u>**To indicate the possessive or genitive case or possession in the**</u>
   <u>**following ways:**</u>

   . <u>When a noun is singular, an apostrophe and **s** are added</u>
      <u>to the noun</u>, e.g.
         . The accountant's office   . Anne's wedding dress
   . <u>An apostrophe and **s** is also added to indefinite pronouns</u>
         <u>that do not end in **s**,</u> e.g.
                  . This is **nobody's** fault.
                  . **Someone's** car is parked in my driveway.
. <u>An apostrophe is added to plural nouns ending in '**s**', e.g.</u>

   . This is a **students'** computer laboratory.
   . Our **doctors'** surgery hours are between 14 –18 hours on Fridays.

. An apostrophe and **s** are added to plural nouns that **do not**
  end in **s**, e.g.
          . There is the young *women's* hockey club.
          . She reads *children's* short stories.
. An apostrophe can be used to show the possessive form without
  mentioning the noun to which a reference is made, e.g.
          . I met John outside the *barber's* (shop).
          . Julie works for a local *optician's* (practice).

You do not have to mention the nouns shown in brackets above.

. An apostrophe is used with some units of measure to denote
  possession, e.g.
          . I think in a *week's* time she will arrive here.
          . My father retired after *forty years'* service as a Civil Servant.
. When a genitive (possessor) consists of more than one noun, the
  apostrophe is marked on the last noun. A genitive shows
  possession, e.g.
          . The British Prime Minister's country residence is not too
            far from London.
          . The Lord Chancellor's office is in the Palace of Westminster.

. When possession is shared by more than one noun, the apostrophe
  and **s** are added to the last noun, e.g.
          . Webster and Lancaster's books can be seen on ADR web site.
          . Brinkman and Blaha's Data Systems And Communications
            Dictionary is a well known book.
. When possession is not shared by more than one noun, the
  apostrophe and **s** are added to each noun, e.g.
          . Earnest's and Klieg's insurance training manuals are in our library.
          . I have Hornby's and Webster's dictionaries.

. Use an apostrophe and **s** with personal names ending with **s** or **z**, e.g.
          . Prince Charles's ideas on the environment are serious.
          . According to Leibniz's Law, if A is identical with B, then every
            property that A has B has, and vice versa.
. An apostrophe and **s** are used with nouns which are preceded
  by the word 'sake', e.g.

. For God's sake, you must not lie during the interview.
. For pity's sake, help your aged and sick parents.

. An apostrophe can be used with plural nouns which are
  preceded by the word 'sake' , e.g.

. For old times' sake, Anne forgave him and invited him for a meal.

If you do something for *old times' sake (idiomatic expression),* you do it
because it is connected with something good that happened to you in the past.

. Use an apostrophe with abbreviations functioning as verbs, e.g.
  . I submitted my application for a day off and my boss *OK'd* it.

$$Ok'd = okayed ↵$$

. In the present tense use 'OK!'. In this context, it means my boss officially
agreed to let me have a day off work. It is rather an informal expression.

. Usually business names do not include an apostrophe in
  their business titles, e.g.

  . I work at Sainsburys.   ⟹ should be Sainsbury's

  . My wife used to work for Browns. ⟹ should be Brown's
. In hyphenated compound words the apostrophe is added to
  the last word, e.g.
      . My wife's brother-in-law's home is not far from our home.
      . A well-dressed lady's car is parked in your place.

2 . **To mark contractions or indicate omissions in**
    spelling certain words, e.g.

              . **We'll** see you soon.
  we will = we'll ↵ also = we shall
              . She **won't** go there today.
      will not = won't ↵

. The following examples also show the use of an apostrophe with
  a pronoun + an auxiliary verb to contract them.

      . I'm = I am   . We're = We are

. They're = They are   . She's = She is **or** She has

In addition to the above, you can find some more common contractions together with their meanings in Table 1.

. **An apostrophe is used to indicate the omission of figures in dates,**
   e.g.
          . They wanted to stay with us in '**04**.
              referring to the year 2004 ↵
          . Thank you for your letter of 9th Jan. '**04**.

Some common contractions

Contraction	Meaning	Contraction	Meaning
aren't	are not	let's	let us
can't	cannot/can not	mustn't	must not
hasn't	has not	she'll	she will/she shall
he's	he is/ he has	there's	there is
he'll	he will/he shall	they'll	they will/they shall
I'd	I would/ I had	they've	they have
it's	it is/it has	weren't	were not
I've	I have	we've	we have
I'll	I will/I shall	you'll	you will/you shall
it's	it is/ it has	you're	you are
		you've	you have

Table 1

. **An apostrophe is not used with the possessive pronouns,** e.g.

          . its   . ours   . yours   . theirs

. **An apostrophe is not used when referring to wars, plans, projects and similar notions related to a specified length of time,** e.g.

. Six-Day War   . Hundred Years' War

this does not obey the rule – exception to the rule

. Five –Year Plan . Ten –Year Projected Savings

There are other exceptions to the above rule.

. **An apostrophe is not used with abbreviations and numbers which create plurals,** e.g.
. the 1980s.
. In the 1950s, she was very young and pretty.

Some writers place it before adding s, e.g. . In the 1950's.
Indeed, there is some controversy surrounding it.

. **An apostrophe is usually used with names of places, when possession is involved,** e.g.

. 12 *St. James's Square* London SW 11.
. *St. John's Wood* Underground station is in London.
. He was seen in the *Earls Court* area yesterday afternoon.

This rule is not always applicable as demonstrated by the last example. Sometimes the insertion or omission of an apostrophe is surrounded by uncertainty.

. **Round brackets or parentheses ( )**

There are several types of brackets. In British English for writing purposes the round brackets ( ) which are known as parentheses are used. Square brackets [ ] are used in the USA. Of course, other types of brackets are used for mathematical and scientific work. Round brackets can perform the following functions:
. to enclose some additional or optional information without affecting the flow and meaning of a sentence, a paragraph or a piece of writing , e.g.

. to show alternatives
. to include abbreviations and refer to something by figures or
  letters

The following example makes it clear:
. Gandhi *(1869-1948)* was the foremost spiritual and political
  leader of the twentieth century. He was called the Mahatma
  (Great Souls – in Sanskrit). Gandhi was a pacifist and a
  great champion of non-violence.

The removal of parentheses and their contents will not affect the flow and
meaning of this paragraph.

(1) . Any student(s) who would like to join this trip must see
         me today.
(2) . Only 2 (two) delegates are allowed free of charge during
         the book fair.

Sometimes in this book, examples are numbered as '(1) ....' ' (2) ....'. The
purpose of this "**.**" is to highlight each example for the ease of the reader.
See the last two examples.

. <u>Square brackets</u> [ ]

Square brackets are used to supplement or append to an original text
some information which may be a correction, an explanation or some
translation by a person other than the author. For instance:

. During the Second World War, the British Prime Minister
  [Churchill] made great and memorable speeches.

----

additional information appended by the editor

. The first woman party leader in British politics
  [Margaret Thatcher] became the longest serving
  20th century female Prime Minister in 1988.

In this case, **[Margaret Thatcher]** is added to the original text by the editor.

. Capital letters

The use of capital letters is governed by the following punctuation rules:

. Use a capital letter at the beginning of a sentence, e.g.

> . Punctuation enables us to write clearly.
> . Use punctuation to improve your writing.

. Use a capital letter after a colon, e.g.

In the following examples, direct speech is within the inverted commas:

. The British Prime Minister, Margaret Thatcher, said:
'I am extraordinarily patient, provided I get my own way
in the end.' (The Observer 4 April 1989)

. Once Mahatma Gandhi said: 'There is enough for the needy
but not for the greedy.'

. Once Goethe (German poet, novelist, and dramatist) said:
'Boldness has genius, power and magic in it.'

. The pronoun I is written as a capital letter, e.g.

> . I'm pleased to meet you.
> . It's a pity I missed your birthday party.

. Use a capital letter to begin a proper noun, e.g.

. Mary is here from York. ⇐ both names begin with capital letters

. Mrs Johnson has arrived. ⇐ both title and surname begin with
capital letter

. A title of a person and proper nouns begin with a capital letter, e.g.

. Dr Robertson is our General Practitioner.
⇑   ⇑   ⇑

title proper name   title made of two words each begin with
a capital letter

. Mrs Taylor will see her **doctor** today.
⇑   ⇑

title   it is not functioning as a title here but
as a common noun

. **Aunt** Kay lives in Nottingham.
⇑

title (Auntie or Aunty is informal for aunt)

. My **aunt** lives in Nottingham but **Uncle** Tom King died some
⇑   ⇑   years ago.
aunt is not a title but   it is the title of Tom King
a common noun

Words like doctor, aunt, grandfather are titles only when they are used with
proper nouns.

. **Nouns for religions, scriptural books and related titles begin with
a capital letter,** e.g.

> . Islam means submission to Allah. A Muslim is someone who
> has submitted to Allah, believing in Muhammad as a prophet
> of Allah. Allah is God in Islam. The Holy Qur'an (also
> known as the Koran) is the holy book of Islam.
> . Christ, the Holy Bible, the Prophet Muhammad, Buddha,
> Judaism, the Talmud, Hindu and Hinduism are all connected
> with different religions.

In the last two examples, Islam, Muslim, Allah, Muhammad, God, the Holy
Qur'an, the Koran, the Prophet Muhammad, the Holy Bible, Buddha, Juda-
ism, the Talmud, Hindu and Hinduism all began with capital letters. Here
these are considered as proper nouns. However, in the phrase 'as a prophet',
prophet is a common noun, not a title. For this reason, it does not begin with
a capital letter.

. Capitals are used to begin the names of places, rivers, mountains,
books, newspapers, plays, films, trains, ships, spacecraft,
aircraft and other such things, e.g.

> . London, Berlin, Moscow and Paris are all capital cities in Europe.
> . The longest span bridge in the world is Akashi-Kaiyo. It is in
> Japan. Its length is 1990 metres.
> . The longest railway tunnel in the world is Seikan, Japan. It is 54 km
> long. The second longest railway tunnel in the world is the
> **Channel Tunnel UK- France**. It is 50 km long.

. The largest desert in the world is the Sahara in northern Africa.

. The highest mountain in the world is Everest in Asia.

. The longest river in the world is the **River Nile** in Africa.

. The largest country in the world by area is **Russia**.

. The largest city by population in the world is **Tokyo** in Japan, Asia.

. The distance from the **Earth** to the **Sun** is about 150 million km.

. The **Himalayas** are the highest mountain range on **Earth**.
  They are mainly in **Pakistan, India, Nepal** and **Bhutan**.

. "The **Times**" is a daily newspaper for well-informed readers in the **UK**.

. "The **Diamond Sūtra**" is the oldest surviving printed book in the world.
  It is a **Chinese** translation of **Buddhist** scripture, printed in AD 868.

. The **Orient Express** is a famous train.

. Apollo 11 made the first lunar landing.

. The actress **Elizabeth Taylor** played the title role in the 1963 film
  "Cleopatra."

. "Java Simplified" is a computer programming book from ADR.

. <u>**Capitals are used for abbreviations of names of some
  organisations and countries. These are formed from the first
  letter of each word in the name**</u>, e.g.

  . **UN** is an abbreviation for the United Nations.

  . **UK** is a short name for the United Kingdom.

  . **EU** stands for the European Union.

  . **BBC** is an abbreviation for the **British Broadcasting** Corporation.

  . **BP** is short for the British Petroleum company.

The correct use of both capital and small letters has been muddled by the arrival of the Internet. Often proper nouns are written either in capital or small letters and joined together. This practice is not recommended in this book.

. <u>**Colon**</u>

A colon is used for the following functions:

. <u>**To introduce a list or a series of items,**</u> e.g.

  . The following students must register their proposals today
    before 16.00 hours: James Walker, Joan Smith, Elizabeth
    Wood and John Baker.

. We can travel to London by any of the three means of travel:
    by car, by train or by coach.

. **To identify a speaker in direct speech and quotations,** e.g.
    . Joy said: 'It was my handbag.'
    . Silvia shouted: 'Leave my home now!'
. **Use a colon for introductory remarks,** e.g.
  . Ladies and gentlemen: allow me to present tonight's guest speaker.

. **To add information to a clause so that it is elaborated,** e.g.
    . This group has students from six countries: Germany,
      Russia, India, China, Ireland and the United Kingdom.
    . We specialise in selling technical books: engineering,
      computing and physical sciences.

. **To supplement information to a phrase so that it is expanded,** e.g.
  . Lots of books: computing, engineering, gardening, short stories, etc.

. **To start a clause which contains an explanation of the previous
clause,** e.g.
    . Today our town is very busy: there is an annual festival
      and a procession along the promenade.
    . Our train was full of overseas visitors: many passengers
      were travelling to London Heathrow Airport.

. **To introduce a subtitle,** e.g.

  . Essential English: <u>Grammar, Structure and Style of Good English.</u>
               subtitle ↵
. <u>To form numerical ratios and other number systems, e.g.</u>
  . Profit and expenditure ratio **4:1**
  . Our train left London Victoria at 15:30 sharp.

. **Another use of the colon is to refer to a document or
correspondence or set the beginning of a letter etc.** For instance:

    <u>From:</u> John Smith   <u>To:</u> James Taylor
    <u>Subject:</u> Delivery by car   <u>Dated:</u> 12.04.2005

. <u>Comma</u>

The comma and full stop are the most common punctuation marks in the English language. The correct use of the comma is not a mystery. Its use is fairly well documented and understood, yet there is a tendency either to use too many commas or to use too few commas in a piece of writing. Indeed, there is a wide variation in the use of commas. Sometimes, a comma as a separator is essential. There are occasions when the use of a comma may be considered as optional for the sake of clarity. The following discussion illustrates its use for some specific purposes:

. <u>List items</u>

. <u>To separate items in a list of three or more items. These items may be words, phrases or clauses,</u> e.g.

. Anne, Wolfgang, Elena and Frank went to Austria for a skiing holiday.
. You can have one more portion of potatoes, peas or cabbage.

<u>Some people insert a comma before the last item in the list, e.g.</u>

> . John is energetic, ambitious, and rich.

<u>However, there is a growing trend towards the omission of the comma before the last item.</u>
. <u>When the last item in the list has **and** in it, the comma is necessary to avoid ambiguity, e.g.</u>
. My children used to enjoy watching television game shows, children's programmes, **and** the **Little and Large** comedy show.
        ⇑   ⇑

        essential comma compound noun –joined by **and**

        conjunction part of the compound noun ↵

. <u>If the list ends with such phrases as 'etc.', 'and the like' and 'so on', a comma is needed to indicate continuity of the same thing, e.g.</u>
  . Gull, golden eagle, finch, duck**, and the like** creatures with feathers and two legs are birds.
  . Tesco, Safeway, Morrison, **etc.** stores have been attracting customers of small corner shops to their own big retail outlets.

. **Clauses**

. To join main clauses if they are linked by the coordinating
  conjunction **and,** *but* or **so,** e.g.
    . Our staff room is situated on the first floor, **and** the students'
      room is on the third floor.
    . You can attend our meeting today, **but** you must not come
      more than five minutes late.

The comma can be omitted when the clauses are short, e.g.
      . She cooks and I clean.
      . We ran very fast but still missed the last bus.
. To separate a subordinate clause or phrase from the main clause,
  the use of a comma may be justified to avoid misunderstanding.
  The comma is more desirable and helpful, when the sentence
  is long, e.g.
    . They returned to their hotel, after three hours of the skiing session.
    . I did not receive my money, at the end of the long working day.

These two sentences may be written without commas.

. **The use of a comma is less common, when the subordinate clause**
  follows the main clause. For this reason, the comma is enclosed
  within the [ ] to indicate that its use is optional, e.g.

    . I did not travel with my wife to London **[,]** because I had to
     attend an important meeting at work.
    . She wrote short stories as well **[,]** so that she could support her family.

. **Use commas to separate an adding clause from the main clause,**
  e.g.
    . My son, who was a soldier , had left the army.
             ⇑ - relative clause
    adding (non-restrictive or non-identifying) clause

If you remove the adding/non-restrictive/non-identifying clause from the sentence, it will still make sense.
    . Miss Jones, who is our store manager, grew up in a foster home.
         adding clause⤶ - relative clause

. No commas are needed to separate identifying (restrictive) and classifying clauses from the main clause. See$\Rightarrow$ clauses

. Use commas to separate the speaker from the direct speech, e.g.
> . The head teacher said, ' No one is allowed to use a mobile phone in class.'
>> . John Smith shouted, 'You are breaking speed limits. Reduce your speed now.'

Single quotation marks are often used to report direct speech. You can also use double quotation marks.

. **Use commas to separate a question tag from the rest of the sentence,** e.g.
. Your wife is a doctor, am I right?
. Your complaint was dealt with by me to your satisfaction, wasn't it?

. **Use commas with numbers in accordance with the following rules:**

. Write non-technical numbers, by placing a comma after every three units, commencing from the right of the number, e.g.

> . 10,000   105, 111, 456   88,000,789
> . The population of Bridlington is around 65,000.

. Often a comma is not used in numbers smaller than 10,000.

There is no need to place commas in these numbers.

Reason: Commas are used with numbers 10,000 and above.

. When dealing with the British currency, the whole pounds should be written with the pound symbol £, e.g.
> . £1   . £5,349   . £24   . £1,009

. When the British currency involves both pounds and pence, write pence in numbers after the decimal point. The comma is also used if the number is £1,000 or greater, e.g.
> . £34 . 05   . £467. 99   . £ 9,789. 75

When the amount is in pounds and pence, do not use the symbol/abbreviation
p for pence. Mixed currency is extended to two places after the decimal point
as shown above. When the amount is less than the whole pound, it is written
as: . 66p   . 99p   . 5p Also written as: . £0 .66 . £0 .99 . £0 .05

Often people write currency in such a preferred way that makes them feel
secure.

. Large amounts involving a million or a billion or a trillion can
  also be written with their respective symbols/abbreviation or
  without it, e.g.
    . **m**   is an abbreviation or a symbol for million
    . **bn** is an abbreviation or a symbol for billion
    . **trillion** is written as trillion
        . 1,000,000 or 1 m   1,000,000,000 or 1 bn
        . 178,000,000 or 178 m   1,500,000,000   or 1.5 bn

. We say a, one, two or several billion or million. There is no need
  to say millions or billions. We say these without the final 's', e.g.

        . At the end of the first six months of this year, our sales reached
          between 2.6 m and 1 bn.

. When there is no quantity or a number before million or
  billion, we say millions or billions, e.g.
        . Millions/billions of pounds were invested in the London Dome.

    You can say:
      . Our government has wasted **tens of millions** on advertising their
        failed policies.   ⇑ - not a figure but a phrase
                                          plural number
      . His grandfather made his **millions** by selling whisky in the USA.

. Always use a plural verb with million or millions and billion
  or billions, e.g.
        . One million **pounds were** spent on this building project.
plural forms of noun + verb ↵
        . Three million **pounds have been** deposited in his bank account.
plural forms of noun + verb ↵

. *Currency in the USA*

Money is written in the same way as pounds and pence in the UK, except with the dollar sign, e.g. . **$ 5,567**   . **$1.6m**   . **$ 10.66**   . **50¢**

. Use commas to separate parenthetic remarks from the rest of the sentence.

Sometimes it is desirable to give additional information by enclosing it in parenthesis <u>by means of a pair of commas</u>. In fact, you can do this by using brackets or dashes. The following examples show the use of parenthesis:

. John's business venture in the USA, **which almost cost him the loss of his family home,** ended with the closure of his business in the USA.

. Mikhail Gorbachev (1931 -), **president of the USSR,** was awarded the Nobel Peace Prize 1990.

. Is parenthetic use of commas is essential?

It is not always necessary, e.g.

  . In the light of the above facts, we, **therefore,** very much appreciate your refund of our deposit . You can re-write it as:

  . In the light of the above facts, we **therefore** very much appreciate your refund of our deposit .

  . I assure you, sir, we will deliver the goods on the agreed date.

<u>You can re-write it as:</u>

  . I assure you, sir we will deliver the goods on the agreed date.

There are some parenthetic phrases such as 'indeed', 'certainly', 'by chance', 'incidentally', etc. These are adverbial elements without parenthetic commas.

. Dash

The prime function of a dash is to separate a part of a sentence from the rest of a sentence. There may be one or more dashes in a sentence. The dash is used for a variety of aims. Some of these are exemplified here:

. In the following examples, dashes have added some excitement and informality:

  . Annabel loved Rex so much — and she left her husband.

  . Here is a bouquet of flowers — my sweetheart.

. **A dash is used** to place emphasis on a **phrase towards the end of a sentence,** e.g.
   . He only has one thing on his mind – his girlfriend.
   . Their car is just six months old – and rather expensive.

. **Dashes are used to separate list items as illustrated below:**
   . All the team members – John, Carl, Carol, Barry, Derek, Elaine and Eva – left.
. **A dash is used to comment on a phrase which preceded it,** e.g.
   . Frankfurt, Vienna and Budapest – these cities are well served by fast trains throughout the year.
   . Just imagine his reaction – he will be furious to see this mess.

. **Dashes are used parenthetically-a pair of dashes must be used,** e.g.
   . The Himalayas – the highest mountains in the world – are the ultimate challenge.
   . Martin Luther King Jr – the US civil-rights campaigner, black leader, and Baptist minister – was awarded the Nobel Peace Prize in 1964.
   . Muhammad Ali – three times World Heavyweight Champion – was the most recognised person in the 20th century in the whole world.

In these examples, a pair of dashes is used instead of brackets in order to enclose the information. This parenthetic use of dashes is equivalent to brackets. For the parenthetic use, a pair of brackets is preferred as information within the brackets stands out better and makes a stronger impression on a reader. Therefore, it is suggested that you avoid using a pair of dashes for brackets.

. **Dashes are used to separate the adding clause from the main clause:**
   . Berlin is smaller than London – where underground trains are too crowded during the rush hours.
   . Charlie Chaplin was a film actor and director – who made his reputation as a tramp with a smudge moustache, bowler hat and twirling cane.

We usually separate the additional clause with commas.

. **A dash is used to indicate different types of ranges,** e.g.
   . World War I 1914 – 1918 caused the death of an estimated
     10 million people.
   . World War II 1939 – 45 caused the loss of an estimated
     55 million lives
. When on both sides of the dash the dates are in the same decade as shown
  above, it is conventional to write only the last two digits on the right side
  of the dash. On the other hand, in the following example, full years/dates
  are given on both sides of the dash because there is a change of century.
          . Queen Victoria 1819 – 1901
          . See pp 210 – 220 **or** See pages 210 – 220
          . A – K
          . volumes I– V

Some writers use dashes to imitate spoken English, to place emphasis, to indicate a missing word or words (maybe a rude word or phrase), incomplete-
ness or uncertainty. Comic writers and tabloid journalists use dashes frequently. In formal writing and in academic work, commas and round brackets
(parentheses) for parenthetic use are generally preferred. It should be noted
that after a dash, only a proper noun begins with a capital letter.

. **Ellipses(dot dot dot)**

Ellipses (singular ellipsis) are a series of usually three full stops,
or points, or dots. In essence, ellipses indicate:
          . omission of one or more words from a sentence
          . a sentence or paragraph is missing from the writing
          . withholding of something for whatever reason
. They were thirsty, but also … and penniless. ⇐ a word (hungry) is
                                                    omitted

. You must tell the panel nothing but … ⇐ a phrase **(the truth)**
                                            is omitted

In the last example, ellipses occurred at the end of the sentence. When ellipses are utilised at the end of a sentence, there is *no* need for the fourth dot or
full stop.

. On the contrary, in the next example, the ellipses are used to separate two complete sentences. In this case, <u>there is a need for the fourth dot.</u> Here ellipses indicate that at least one complete sentence has been withheld. The missing or withheld sentence or further sentences should have been where ellipses are shown.

. <u>I have never said that</u> **...** . <u>I don't use that sort of language.</u>
         1   ⇑   2

complete sentence   ellipses   complete sentence

. They visited us in 1996,1997, 1998 ... ⇐ subsequent years omitted

. **Exclamation mark !**

The exclamation mark is represented by !. It is a terminator just like the full stop; but it is used for the following specific purposes.

. <u>**To indicate strong emotional feelings** – **anger, happiness, sorrow, surprise, etc.**</u> For instance:
> . How wonderful the party was!
> . Didn't they cry!
> . We won! Hurrah!

. <u>**To mark emphatic phrases - scorn, insult, swearing, irony,] command,** etc</u>. For instance:
> . She must be silly!   . You're a mess!
> . Get out of my class! And wait outside until I call you back!
> . Get lost!

. <u>**To mark the end of interjections**</u> , e.g.
> . Cheers! . Blimey! . Be quiet! . Ow! (Ow! That hurt me!)

. <u>**To indicate the importance of a specific statement**</u> , e.g.
> . What a difficult journey she faced!
> . Didn't I call your name? Sorry!
> . John is only twelve!

. <u>**Some other uses of exclamation marks**</u>:

Sometimes people use multiple exclamation marks in order to make a piece of writing more interesting. Unless you are writing comic material or working for the tabloid press, try not to use them. In mathematics, the exclamation stands for the factorial sign. e.g., five factorial = 5!. As a matter of interest, its value works out as: **5!** = (5x4x3x2x1) = 120.

. **Footnotes**

A footnote is written below the text at the bottom of the page. It may be an explanation, a comment, some additional information or a reference. The most common symbol used for footnotes is the Indo-Arabic numeral written as a superscript figure. A superscript number/figure is written above the normal line of writing. For instance:

> . "Object Oriented Programming (OOP) is not new. What is new is the application of its concepts in modern programming languages such as C++ and Java."[1]

> 1 Java Simplified, Adam Shaw, ADR, 1999.

Some people use some other symbols such as asterisks and oblique.

. **Full stop**

The full stop is the most commonly used punctuation mark. It is also known as **full point**. In the United States of America, it is called **period**. It is a terminator that is used for a variety of situations as exemplified below:

. Rose is engaged to Russell. ⇐ full stop at the end of a sentence

. Would you kindly leave this room now. ⇐ a polite request

. May I ask you to show me your current pass. ⇐ a polite request

Note that polite requests are not questions and thus a full stop is placed at the end of each statement.

. What you should do is to listen to your mother.⇐ a recommendation

. <u>Use a full stop at the end of indirect speech that sounds like a question,</u> e.g.

> . I would very much like to know where your manor in Yorkshire is.
> . The office manager wanted to find out why the monthly report was delayed.

. <u>Many abbreviations end with a full stop,</u> e.g.

> . Joan Smith Ph.D.
> . Dr. A .Williams is away this week.

There is a tendency not to place full stops after initials. Some people <u>do not</u> use the full stop at the end of any abbreviation. For instance:

. Jan ⇐ January . It should be Jan.

. e. g ⇐ for example . It should be e.g.

. <u>The abbreviation **e.g.** is derived from the Latin words
EXEMPLI GRATIA.</u>

. **et al.** - <u>it means 'and other people or things'.</u> It is derived from
the Latin **'et alii or alia'** or **'aliae'** . It is usually used after names,
e.g. . discovered by John Major et al., 2001

. **etc.** – <u>it means in the list there are other items that could</u> <u>have been
included.</u> It is an abbreviation for **et cetera** **or et ceteri**, e.g.
Colin, Robin, Jane, etc.

.The **U.N.** offices in the **U.K.** are in London. ⇐ the UN offices in
the UK are in London

. <u>**Use full stops for both British and American currencies,**</u> e.g.

. £45.<u>76</u>   ⇐ pounds . pence

seventy-six pence↵

. $ 45.<u>90</u>   ⇐ dollars . cents

ninety cents↵

In both examples, the full stop is used as a <u>**symbol for the decimal point.**</u> In
the UK, <u>less than a pound is usually</u> written as a number with p, e.g. 96p.

. <u>**No full stop is added to abbreviations for metric measurements,**</u>
e.g.   cm ⇒ centimetre   mm ⇒ millimetre
km ⇒ kilometre   mg ⇒milligram

. <u>**Full stops are used between days, months and years when dates
are written in numbers,**</u> e.g. . 01.05. 04   . 31.03.2005

. <u>**A full stop is placed between the hours and minutes when time is
written in the UK. There is a full stop after m in p.m.,**</u> e.g.

. 3.45 <u>**a.m.**</u>   . 8.15 <u>**p.m.**</u>

ante meridiem ↵ also am   post meridiem ↵ - also pm

. ante meridiem $\Rightarrow$ before noon. It is from Latin$\Rightarrow$ **ante meridiem**

. post meridiem $\Rightarrow$after noon. It is from Latin$\Rightarrow$ **post meridiem**

. **A full stop is placed at the end of a footnote irrespective of its grammatical status,** e.g.

.   1 pp. 12-33.   . 2 Adam Shaw in Java, pp. 10-12.

Note that **pp.** is an abbreviation for pages. It is written in lower-case letters followed by a full stop. A **lower-case** abbreviation cannot begin a sentence.

. Hyphen

It can be said that hyphens are used for two main functions:

. to join two words together
. to split the word at the end of a line of print

In British English, hyphens are more commonly used than in American English. The following examples illustrate some of the purposes for using hyphens.

. He went to see his **mother-in-law** in the Bahamas.

⇑ - compound noun containing a preposition
hyphen forming a compound noun

. The following examples also demonstrate the use of the hyphen
in forming compound words:

. He is a **jack-of-all-trades** who takes on almost any work
he is offered.

. You can travel by an *inter-city* train anywhere in France.

. His *ex-wife* is a hairdresser.

. She paid **seventy-seven** pounds for this beautiful dress.

Compound numbers – remember!

1. The hyphen is used in writing out numbers in words between
twenty-one and ninety-nine.
2.   Do not use hyphens when writing out numbers in words such as
three hundred.
3. In compound numbers hundred, thousand, etc. do not end with –s.

For instance:
  . Your bill comes *to* **two hundred** and **thirty-four** pounds.

. <u>**The following examples show that when a compound word is**</u>
  <u>**formed with a verb form, it is written with a hyphen:**</u>
      . John couldn't think of a **put-down** fast enough.
      . Natasha gave a **record-breaking** performance last night.
      . It is a **well-thought-out** idea.
      . Barbara is always well-dressed.
The use of the hyphen in compound words is often debatable.

. <u>**The following examples illustrate that some nouns preceded by a**</u>
  <u>**letter are hyphenated:**</u>
    . On British motorways a **U-turn** is prohibited.
    . Our hospital is short of chest **X-ray** machines.

. <u>**The following examples show that some compound nouns**</u>
  <u>**with adverbs or prepositions are usually written with or without**</u>
  <u>**hyphens:**</u>
            . motorway *or* motor-way
            . turn-over **or** turn over
. <u>**The following examples show that in some words with prefixes,**</u>
  <u>**hyphens are used to separate the prefix from the root word:**</u>

    . Our home telephone number is <u>**ex - directory**</u>.
              prefix ⏎   ⇑
                              root word
  . A **post-dated** cheque will be treated as payable immediately.

. <u>**The following examples demonstrate that adjective compounds**</u>
  <u>**preceded by *self* are hyphenated:**</u>

  . The enclosed document is **self-explanatory**.
  . In some Indian villages, **self-help** community projects have
        transformed villagers' lives.
  . Last summer, we rented a **self-contained** flat in a small sea-side
        town in France.
  . Don't be too **self-critical** because such an attitude can be **self-destructive**.

. Professor Burkhardt is a **self-styled** professor of the
  German language.
. He is a **self-taught** software designer.
. Kay always seems so calm and **self-possessed**.
. You shouldn't allow fear and **self-doubt** to rule your life.

Here are Some Compound words = self+ hyphen +root word:
⇓

self-access, self-appointed, self-appraisal, self-assertive, self-assured,
self-awareness, self-catering, self-centred, self-confessed,
self-confident, self-congratulation, self-conscious, self-contradiction,
self-control, self-criticism, self-deception, self-defeating,
self-defence, self-denial, self-destruction, self-determination,
self-discipline, self-drive, self-educated, self-employed, self-esteem,
self-evident, self-examination, self-fulfilling, self-government,
self-image, self-important, self-imposed, self-indulgent, self-inflicted,
self-interest, self-made, self-opinionated, self-pity, self-preservation,
self-reliant, self-respect, self-restraint, self-righteous, self-sacrifice,
self-satisfied, self-seeking, self-service, self-serving, self-worth.

. **Hyphens are also used in double-barrelled family names as
  illustrated below:**
      . Mr. and Mrs. **Douglas-Home** are here.
      . Lord *Baden-Powell* founded the Boy Scout movement in 1908.

Note that the first letter in each double-barrelled name begins with a
capital letter.

. **Some British names of places are also hyphenated,** e.g.
      . **Southend-on-Sea** is in Essex near London.
      . **Stratford-upon-Avon** is where William Shakespeare was
        born in 1564.

The word after the preposition begins with a capital letter as illustrated
above. In these days, due to the advent of the Internet, the growing trend is to
ignore hyphens in names of places.

. **Hyphens at the end of a line (word division)**

We are in the age of Information Technology (IT). Typewriters have virtually been replaced by keyboards and word-processors. Generally speaking, word-processing software truncates a word at the end of a line in accordance with its own rule. Increasing numbers of books are created by using word-processing software. It is the word-processor which formats the document, hence inserts the hyphen at the point of a word division at the end of a line. This is shown below:

'There are two subject areas, namely **etymology** and **phonetics**, which deserve mention here. **Etymology** is the study of word origin and **phonetics** is the study of speech and sounds. **Etymology** has a set of rules for dividing the word into syllables, prefixes and suffixes. Phonetics suggests the division of a word based on its sounds. If you are keen to explore word division, it is suggested that you pay a visit to your local library to consult reference books or search the Internet for further **information** on these topics.'

. <u>Paragraph</u>

There are no hard-and-fast rules that regulate a paragraph's size and content. In any piece of writing, paragraphs enable the writer to lay the text in its most appropriate order so that the reader is at ease with the text. A paragraph contains a main theme. The main theme may have one or more related points. The whole idea is to place related points in a paragraph so that the reader is helped to grasp what is being written. Of course, the main theme may have several related paragraphs.

For instance, the main theme of the above section is the use of the hyphen. It has two related paragraphs. The first paragraph talks about the way words are divided by a word-processor these days. In the second paragraph, an example is given in order to demonstrate how the word-processor has divided two words **phonetics** and **information** at the end of two lines (see above).

These paragraphs are short and concise. In fact, the length of a paragraph is dictated by the amount of the text in the main theme and related points. As in this example, the sizes of both paragraphs are based on the amount and flow of the text in each paragraph.

Some people write long paragraphs. For instance, a letter from a solicitor (lawyer) usually has long paragraphs. There are other experts such as philosophers who also construct longer paragraphs as longer paragraphs provide them with plenty of space to develop their ideas and argue their opinions.

Nowadays, the widespread tendency is to write shorter paragraphs.

Paragraphs are also visual aids. Some writers prefer to leave at least one blank line between two paragraphs. This is the style of this book. Some writers have other preferences. For instance, they start a paragraph by indenting the first word by a number of letter spaces, usually 3 to 5. They do not allow a blank line between two paragraphs. Hardly ever, writers indent and allow a blank line space at the same time. If you are interested in fiction and poetry, consult some relevant reference materials for paragraphing techniques. It is worth mentioning that publishers have their own house style for paragraphing.

. Question mark ?

The question mark (**?**) is a terminator like the full stop. The main purposes for which it is used are exemplified below:

. **The following examples elucidate that what precedes the question mark is an interrogative sentence,** e.g.
  . Are you related to this woman?
  . What are you carrying in that heavy suitcase?
  . The policeman asked me first, 'Is this your car?'
  . I asked him, 'Where were you at the time of the accident?'

The purpose of the interrogative question is to get an answer from the respondent. An interrogative question or a **direct question** always ends with a question mark.

. **A direct 'question-like' statement ends with a question mark(question tag),** e.g.
  . It is a lovely morning, isn't it ?
  . She looks very pretty in her wedding dress, doesn't she?
  . They look disappointed, don't they?
  . Joan's mother is always nagging her, isn't she?

. The following example shows that instead of asking a full question, you can make it short. **The short question also ends with a question mark:**
  . What is your name? ⇒ short form ⇒ First name please?

. What is your surname? $\Rightarrow$ short form $\Rightarrow$ Surname please?

. What is your home telephone number? $\Rightarrow$ short form $\Rightarrow$ Home
                                                                     telephone please?

. What is your permanent address? $\Rightarrow$ short form $\Rightarrow$ Permanent
                                                                     address please?

The above example (it is just one example) illustrates that a short question can be a short phrase(a phrase may be just one word, e.g. run!).

. **When there is uncertainty about a fact, a question mark is usually used to point it** , e, g.
   . Socrates (?470 –399 BC) was a Greek philosopher.
   . Friedrich Engels (?1820-95) was a German philosopher who
     collaborated with Karl Marx on The Communist
     Manifesto (?1848).
   . Albert Einstein was born in Berlin(?).

Often a date or place of birth is doubtful or unverified.

. **The question mark is not used with an indirect question,** e.g.
   . We would like to know what your thoughts are on capital
     punishment.
   . I was wondering if you could give my wife a lift to the
     town centre.
   . We would like to know what the cost is.

. **In chess, the question mark is used by itself and with other symbols**, e.g.
          . ? means a bad move   . ?? stands for a serious blunder

. Some writers use two question marks (??) or a question mark
   with an exclamation mark (?!) to imply scepticism or strong
   feelings, e.g.
            . Do you really think he is telling us the truth??
            . What made you believe her??

Some people repeat question marks several times with or without the exclamation mark. **The use of more than one question mark is not recommended for formal writing.**

. Quotation marks

Quotation marks are also known as inverted commas, speech marks and quotes. There are single quotation marks (' ') as well as double quotation marks (" "). In Britain, single quotes are preferred. The main purposes of using quotation marks are exemplified below:

. Direct speech

It is someone's exact spoken words. When direct speech is reported or quoted, the words actually spoken must be within quotation marks. The writer must also give the precise source of the words actually spoken. The reader should know to whom quoted words are attributed. For instance:

- . 'How do you like the flowers I sent you through Interflora?' Mr. Blair asked his wife.
- . 'War is always a sign of failure,' said the President of France.
- . 'We will always remember Jill as a kind person,' said Mrs. Jones. 'she was ever so friendly and generous to us.'

This example illustrates:

a) when a quoted speech is interrupted at the end of a sentence, instead of a full stop a comma is used to mark the end of the sentence, and

b) the word which resumes the quoted speech begins with a small letter.

. When words 'where', 'why', 'yes' and 'no' are part of direct speech, these are enclosed within quotation marks (but not in reported speech), e.g.
   - . Veronica said to him, 'Yes!'
   - . 'Yes,' Tom replied, but Monica shouted, 'No! It is not for me.'
   - . Joyce asked, 'Where?'
   - . Gary said, 'Why?'
   - . When we asked him to come along with us, he replied, **'No.'**

. Indirect speech

When instead of reporting someone's exact words, the meaning of words is expressed in the third person form using the past tense, e.g.

- When we asked Derek to travel with us, he said no.

- She has just left home. She did not say where she was going.

You do not use quotation marks with reported speech
- When a quotation is within another quotation, double quotation
  marks are used to enclose the quotes within quotes, e.g.

  - 'What do you mean by **"late"**?' I asked him.
  - I asked the speaker, 'Could you please give an example of
    "willy-nilly"?'

In this last example, **willy-nilly** is a quote within a quote. It is an adverb (informal use). It means irrespective of whether someone wants to or not, e.g.
we were forced willy-nilly by the policeman to turn left. It also means doing
something carelessly without planning or thinking, e.g.

  - She spends her money willy-nilly.

- When the direct quotation has several paragraphs, it is customary to
  start each paragraph with an opening quotation mark, and place
  the closing quotation mark at the end of the entire quotation, e.g.

  - 'Tagore also believed in learning by doing. For this purpose, a
    garden and a handicraft shop were part of his school. He had
    great interest in ecological matters. He used to have tree
    planting ceremonies.

  'Tagore also founded a university. At his university, he established
  an international faculty in order to teach unity in diversity.'

  (Rabindranath Tagore – the first Asian to
  receive the Nobel Prize for Literature 1913)

- **When a phrase or a word is quoted, it is enclosed within
  quotation marks,** e.g.
- Colin told me 'certainly no deal', which I conveyed to my boss.
- My doctor declared my health was 'excellent'.

- Titles of lectures, book chapters, articles, short stories and short
  poems, television and radio programmes and musical writing
  are shown in quotes, e.g.

. The title of our annual lecture is ' The Role of Neighbourhood Watch'.

. 'Fruit Gathering' is one of Rabindranath Tagore's poems.

- **The following rules should be observed for quotes:**

a) . Punctuation marks (comma, full stop, question mark, etc.) connected with quoted words are placed **inside the closing quotation mark**, e.g.

- . 'I am fine. How is your wife?' he said to me.

- . 'We have been trying to compromise for three days. Can someone suggest another idea which may appeal to all of us? Let's see who has a bright idea. First, let's have a drink!' the chairman remarked.

b) . When a statement or a sentence finishes with a quotation that ends with a full stop, or a question mark, or an ellipsis, or an exclamation mark, the full stop to stop the entire statement is not required, e.g.

- . She said, 'I sent you my CV yesterday.'

- . Sarah shouted, 'It's marvellous!'

- . Alan said to his wife, ' I never agreed to your … '

- . My teacher asked me, 'How long do you need to finish this essay?'

c) . Punctuation marks (comma, full stop, question marks, etc.) connected with the entire sentence are placed outside the closing quotation marks, e.g.

- . A few days ago, I read a book ' Napoleon Bonaparte – The French Emperor'.

- . I wrote a letter to a friend and told her about 'White Teeth' by Zadie Smith.

. <u>Semicolon</u>

A semicolon (;) indicates that there are two separate pieces of information in a sentence. It is used for the following purposes:

. <u>To join two related clauses:</u>

> . Alexander is a well-known local businessman; he is also mayor.
> . Anne went to Austria from Frankfurt; she stopped en route
>   in Stuttgart for a few hours.

In these examples, clauses could have been joined by '**and**' a coordinating conjunction. You can also write each example as two separate short sentences, ending each with a full stop. A semicolon, like the full stop, indicates that these are separate but related short sentences.

. <u>To join clauses that are linked by a conjunction in order to place greater emphasis on the following clause,</u> e.g.

> . All motor cars must be fitted with seatbelts; and both the
>   driver and passengers must fasten their seatbelts correctly.
> . It is not true to say that poverty is man-made; but it is the result
>   of many complicated and inter-related factors.

. <u>To separate groups within a list which may have a number of commas in each group,</u> e.g.

> . We publish computer programming, information technology
>   and English language books; we represent American and
>   Australian medical, engineering and science books publishers;
>   we also supply technical, medical and IT periodicals through the
>   post to our regular subscribers both at home and abroad.

> . You should demonstrate both written and spoken working
>   knowledge of German and French; explain how European Union
>   laws are incorporated and implemented at governmental levels
>   in France and Germany; and the way industry and commerce
>   operate in these countries.

In these examples, semicolons have created groups within the list. The elements in each group are separated by commas. In essence, semicolons

---

eliminate the overuse of coordinating conjunctions and refine long sentences
by balancing them well.

. **To create a pause when preceded by an adverb or conjunction**
  such as 'nevertheless', 'moreover', 'hence', 'besides', 'also',
  'consequently', ' that is to say', e.g.

>   . In city centres car speed is limited; moreover, honking your
>   car horn aimlessly is prohibited.
>   . She is really self-motivated; hence, she always completes her
>   task on time.
>   . Elizabeth is friendly, rich and generous ; therefore she has
>   many friends.

. Slash

A slash functions as a separator. It is also known as bar, diagonal, oblique
mark, solidus, and stroke. Some of its uses are as follows:

. **To indicate alternatives,** e.g.

>   . Tea/Coffee   ⇐ instead of **or** a slash is used
>   . Dear Sir/Madam (may be ended with or without a comma)
>   . We vote now/adjourn the meeting for lunch.
>   . True/False
>   . He/she can stand for the election of club secretary.

. **To indicate fiscal (connected with the government's financial**
  year), academic, accounting and similar fixed periods of time, e.g.

>   . Tax Year 2004/05
>   . Academic year 2004/05
>   . Balance Sheet for the Period 2003/04

. **To form part of certain abbreviations,** e.g.

>   . I/O   – output in the computing world
>   . A/C No. 1200   – Account = A/C
>   . Send it to me c/o John Smith   – c/o = care of

. The slash is also used for some specific purposes in scientific, technical and
  Information Technology (IT) fields. It has two forms in IT. These are a
  forward slash (/) and a backslash(\). Personal Computers and Internet users
  deal with these types on a regular basis.

. <u>Asterisk</u>

The symbol for the <u>**asterisk**</u> is a star **(*)**. It is used for the following purposes:

. <u>To indicate a reference, a footnote or an explanation given at the</u>
<u>bottom of the text or elsewhere on the same page, e.g.</u>

     . First-degree burns affect the very top layer of the skin.*

         * Hazel Courtney with Gareth Zeal in
            500 of the Most Important Health Tips 2001

<u>Some people prefer to use superscript numbers instead of the asterisk.</u>

. <u>**To indicate omission of letters in taboo words,**</u> e.g.

     . He is really a gentle person who rarely loses his temper.
       He was understandably annoyed and shouted, 'F *** off!'

. <u>**To show the importance of a particular word or phrase,**</u> e.g.

     . The items out of stock are marked with an asterisk and
should be re-order by tomorrow:

         ISBN 19011 97808
         ISBN 1901197 883*
         ISBN 1901197 999
         ISBN 1901197 700*

. <u>**Word-processing symbols (or marks)**</u>
<u>**(bullets, bolds, italics, underlining and arrows, etc.)**</u>

We are in the age of IT and increasingly using word-processors. There are many symbols now that were not available on typewriters. These symbols or marks should be used sensibly as they can make your writing lively and readable.

<u>**Bullets**</u> have been increasingly appearing in printed material. In this book bullets are used in order:

. To begin a heading so that it can stand out as the start of another section.

. To form part of numbering system for examples.

. To show the importance of the text to follow.

. To summarise points made or show conclusions.

. To use bold, italics, underlining techniques, and arrows which can help the reader in the following ways:

. **Bolds, italics, underlining and arrows are used for the following functions:**

. To highlight the importance of a word, phrase, or a larger piece of text by means of **bold,** *italics* and underlining tools.

. To pinpoint a particular word, phrase, or a clause in a sentence by means of an arrow (⇐ ⤶ ⇓). In many places in this book, this technique is applied.

. To clarify the pinpointed text by giving further information on its nature and function. You can also make the pinpointed text larger so that it can stand out.

These techniques can only be applied if you use a word-processor. These are very useful tools when the writer wants the reader to easily comprehend the idea being introduced and discussed. These means of marking text are new and on the periphery of punctuation. With the passage of time, they will be well recognised and used, especially by science, technical, and text books writers. Use them if you think they will help you clarify the text.

In summary, punctuation marks enable us to join, separate, and manipulate words, phrases, clauses, and paragraphs. In addition, these marks can enhance the meaning of a piece of writing irrespective of its size.

Part 3
Troublesome Words and Phrases

The purpose of this part is to describe some common words and phrases which often confuse some writers. These are listed here in **an A-Z order**.

. <u>**a/an**</u> – these are indefinite articles (determiners).
. <u>Which form of the indefinite article should be used before a word?</u>
. <u>Which form of the indefinite article comes before a word beginning with the letter *h*?</u>

The use of these indefinite articles largely depends on the pronunciation of the initial letter of a word. The following guidelines will help you to grasp when to use a correct indefinite article.

a) When a word begins with a consonant sound then '**a**' comes before the word. For instance:

     . a room   . a chair   . a picture   . a road
     . a shop   . a triangle   . a prince   . a car

b) It is not the spelling of a word that determines which form of the article should be used before a word. Therefore, when a word begins with a vowel but sounds as a consonant, it is by preceded by the indefinite article '**a**'. It is exemplified below:

       . A **u**nion of old friends . The minute is a **u**nit of time.
In both examples, '**u**' sounds like the consonant '**y**'.

c) When the initial letter of a word sounds as one of the five vowels (a, e, i, o, u), then the indefinite article '**an**' is placed before the word. Here are some examples:

         . an apple   . an egg   . an ink pot   . an old coat   . an uncle

         . She has **an u**nderwater camera for her work.

         . John is **an e**xperienced teacher.

d) <u>**In the old days**</u> the initial letter '**h**' was not pronounced . It meant that a word began with the letter '**h**' was preceded by the indefinite article '**an**'. For instance:

. an hotel ⇒ it was pronounced as **'otel'**

. an history book ⇒ history was pronounced as **'istory'**

.In fact, even today, the use of **an** before some words beginning with the
  letter **'h'** is still recommended by some quality dictionaries. For example:

. **an** honour   . **an** heir   . **an** heiress   . **an** heirloom

. **an** honest person   . **an** honorary post   . **an** honourable lady

. We took about **an h**our to get here by car.

. In some quality dictionaries, you will find that placing **'an'** before some
  words which begin with the letter **'h'** is described as old-fashioned.
  Why is it so?

This is in accordance with the old practice, when the initial **'h'** was not pronounced, and if the next letter in the word was a consonant, the word was
preceded by **an**. Some people still begin the word with the consonant **h**, then
do not pronounce it. Today, this practice is considered as old-fashioned, e.g.

. **an** hysterical laughter ⇒ it should be ⇒ a hysterical laughter

. **an** horrendous experience ⇒ it should be ⇒ a horrendous experience

. **an** hallucination - Is this figure real or just **an** hallucination?

         it should be **a h**allucination↵

. The good news is that if you examine some quality dictionaries, you will
  discover only a few words beginning with the letter **'h'** which should be
  preceded by the indefinite article **an**. On the other hand, there are only
  a handful words which begin with the letter **'h'** and which are preceded by
  'an', where the letter **h** is not pronounced. In fact, most words beginning
  with the letter **'h'** are preceded by the indefinite article **'a'**. For instance:

. It has a **h**armonious combination of colours.   . **a** history book

. **a** half-moon   . He has **a h**orror of speaking in public

. This town needs **a h**ostel for the growing number of homeless.

. a bit

It means slightly, a little or to a small extent. It is used as an adverb as
illustrated below:

. Joan's new shoes were **a bit** tight.

. I am about to leave home. Please wait **a bit** for me.

. In informal English, it is used to mean a large amount of something.

. How much did you pay for this new car? **Quite a bit**.

. How much was your monthly salary at that time ? **Quite a bit.**

. a bit of (something)

It means the same as **a little**. It is used informally. For instance:
> . Have you go anything else to do this afternoon? Yes,
> I would like to do **a bit of shopping**.
> . Can you give me **a bit of paper** to write down your new postcode?
> . How do you like your new job?
> I think it will **take a bit of** getting used to my new surroundings.

. a few

It means a small quantity of something, or a small number of people, etc.
> . I was pleased to meet **a few** old colleagues at our staff annual party.
> . I have seen only **a few** historical places in your country.

It is worth mentioning that in idiomatic English, **quite a few** and **a good few** mean not a small number, but rather **a large number** (**few** can be used without **a**). For instance:
> . In our large company, a good number of older employees will
> retire soon.
> . There were **quite a few** new members at the meeting.

. a good(or great) deal of (something)

It refers to a large number or a lot of something . For instance:
> . Our local government has spent **a great deal of money** on this project.
> . **A good deal of effort** has gone into making this event a great success.
> . My car will take **a good deal of petrol** for this long journey to Scotland.

. a handful of (something)

It just the opposite of a good/great deal of something. It means a small number of something:
> . Our train was full and **a handful of our colleagues** had to wait for
> . Only **a handful of carrots** are in the basket. Let's buy some more.

. a large number of (something)

It means big/many in size or quantity:
> . **A large number of students** boycotted classes today in protest.
> . He was declared bankrupt in the High Court , because he owed **a large sum of money** to his business creditors.

. a little

It means the same as **a few.** It can be used without **a.** It often means small:
   . My grandmother is **a little lady** who is wearing a red headscarf.
   . There was **little demand** for our service in that town.

. abbreviations

An abbreviation is a shortened or contracted form of a word or a phrase. When an abbreviations is formed from the first and the last letters of a word, it is known as a **contraction**. For example:

. Mr ⟹ an abbreviation (contracted form) for Mister

. Dr ⟹ an abbreviation (contracted form) for Doctor

. When an abbreviation consists of several letters, no full stop is used, e.g.
      . BBC (not B. B. C.) . MP (not M. P.)   . Yorks
      . MSc   . BSc   . BA

The modern trend is not to use full stops with abbreviations. However, some people still prefer the use of a full stop. For instance:

      . Dr.   . St. ⟹ an abbreviation for **street** or **Saint**
It is a matter of taste rather than a rigid universally accepted rule.

. It is still worth mentioning that abbreviations which are formed with the first letter and one or more other letters usually have a full stop, e.g. **Prof.** is an abbreviation for the word Professor. Some abbreviations are formed from Latin words with a full stop or full stops.
. The plural form of an abbreviation in most cases is formed by adding a small 's' to the abbreviation, e.g. **Drs** for doctors), **Sts** for streets or Saints.
. The abbreviations for weights and measurements are written in small letters and mostly take the same(with some exceptions) form for both singular and plural. Here are some examples:
   . kg . km . mm   . cm . lb(pound) . oz (ounce)
   . gal (gallon) . kw (also k**W**) for measuring electrical power

There are some exceptions to this rule. For instance, in the following examples, a small **'s'** is added to the singular forms to make them plural.
   . hrs (hours) . mins (minutes) . secs (seconds) . yrs (years)

. Which form of the indefinite articles 'a' and 'an' should be used
  before an abbreviation?

The use of a correct indefinite article before an abbreviation is
somewhat confusing.

Mister (Mr) and Doctor(Dr) and are pronounced as full words but written out
in short form as abbreviations. These and most other abbreviations do not
have their own distinct pronunciation, because they sound just like full words
when spoken.

Another well-known abbreviation is **VIP (Very Important Person**). This
abbreviation is pronounced as the sound of three different letters.
Indeed, the choice of the indefinite article depends on the pronunciation of
the initial letter of the abbreviation. The following guidelines will help you to
use the correct form of the indefinite article before an
abbreviation:
a) If the abbreviation begins with a consonant sound, use **a** before the
     abbreviation. For instance:

> . **a** PC ⟹ personal computer   . **a** PhD document

> . **a** VIP treatment   . **a** St ⟹ Street or Saint also Station

. **a** PAYE system in the UK ⟹ Pay as you earn income tax system

b) If the abbreviation begins with a vowel sound, use **an** before the
     abbreviation. For example:

> . **an** MSc degree ⟹ here m is pronounced as **em**

> . **an** SAS ⟹ Special Air Service

> . **an** oz ⟹ ounce(s) – a unit of measurement for measuring weights

> . **an** sae ⟹ stamped addressed envelope or self-addressed envelope

c) If the abbreviation begins with a vowel but it sounds like **'y'**
     or **'w'**, use **'a'** before the abbreviation. Here are some examples:

> . **a** UN peacekeeping force   . a u-boat   . a **E**uro-MP

> . an **MP** ⟹ a Member of Parliament (of British Parliament)
> . Tom **&** I went to France in 2004.
>   ⇑

do not use it in the middle of a sentence

. ability to...

It should be used for someone's acquired skills for doing something:

> . He has **the ability to** teach computer programming as well as
> Roman History.
> . Her **ability to dance** well was admired by millions of TV
> viewers.

If you want to refer to someone's inborn talent see ⟹ **capacity for---**

. absurd and ridiculous

It should be used to mean wholly/completely beyond rational thinking and
common sense. It places a much stronger emphasis than the word ridiculous.
For instance:

> . Your story is untrue. What **an absurd** plan!
> . It is absurd to say that in some communist countries people
>   were contented. On the contrary, they were brutally suppressed.

See ⟹ ridiculous

. abuse and misuse

Both words mean the same, that is incorrect, wrong or improper but they are
used in different contexts. **Abuse** is used when you want to say that someone
has incorrectly, improperly, unjustly or excessively used one's official or
privileged position. It shows condemnation or very strong disapproval, e.g.

> . At present, the Home Secretary is being **accused of abusing** his
>   status by giving two free rail tickets to his former lover.

. It is also used for expressing unfair treatment of children or old people, e.g.

> . Occasionally the media highlights the **abuse of children** in some
>   childcare homes.

. It also describes offensive, insulting or rude remarks, violence or sexual
assault and the use of drugs which are health hazards, e.g.

> . Our polite discussion on the current economy turned into a heated
>   debate and John shouted abuse at me.
> . It is reported in some national newspapers that a top civil
>   servant sexually abused his female colleague at the annual
>   staff party.

. Some young people abuse their bodies with drugs like heroin.
. She told us that she had suffered years of physical abuse.

See ⇒ misuse

. academic

The meaning of **'academic'** depends very much on the context in which it is being used.

. In these days, outside the educational world, it is used to imply that something is theoretical rather than practical or it is unimportant or irrelevant, e.g.

   . There is not enough time to complete this test match between England and India. The whole thing's **academic** now. let's go home.
   . Two-thirds of constituencies have already declared their results in favour of the Labour Party, making it the winner. Whether Labour will win or not in a handful of districts, where the results have yet to be declared, is **academic**.
. In the educational world, academic is both a noun and an adjective. If you **use it as a noun,** e.g.   . He is an **academic**.

It means he is a teacher or a researcher at a university or a college of higher education. If you use it before a noun, it functions **as an adjective,** e.g.
. My son left home for the start of his first **academic year** at Leeds University.

. accountable (to or for something)

In the main, it means responsible, but it has a much stronger emphasis than the word responsible (see responsible). It is used when you have done something serious and are asked by someone in authority to explain your action or decision of doing so. It is usually used in cases such as:
   . Police think that the suspect held in their custody is **accountable for** organising last night's disturbances in the local shopping centre.
   . In a democratic country, politicians are **accountable to** the voters.
   . It was obvious that she was **accountable for** causing this fatal accident because her car was driven on the wrong side of the motorway.

. acquaint(–somebody /yourself with something)

It means to become familiar yourself with somebody or something. It creates a spelling problem for many people, as the common error is to omit **c.** It is a verb and the noun is **acquaintance,** which also causes the same common spelling error. An acquaintance is someone whom you know but he/she is not your close friend. Here are some examples of their usage:

- . I am not yet acquainted with this new database system.
- . When you arrive in Paris, you have to acquaint yourself with their Metro/underground rail system.
- . I'm afraid, we do not have a wide circle of friends and acquaintances in this town.
- . Mr. Booth is my business acquaintance.

. acronyms

Acronyms are formed from the first letters of some words that make up the name or title of an organisation or whatever. Just to remind you that an abbreviation is pronounced as a series of letters. Unlike abbreviations, acronyms are pronounceable nouns. For instance:

- . NATO for the ⇒ **North Atlantic Treaty Organization**

- . UNESCO for the ⇒**U**nited **N**ations **E**ducational, **S**cientific and **C**ultural **O**rganization

Acronyms are written in capital letters without full stops as shown above. The use of the indefinite article depends on the initial letter of an acronym. If it begins with the vowel sound, **an** comes before it, otherwise **a,** e.g.

- . **an** UNESCO conference   ⇐ u is a vowel – thus the vowel sound
- . **a** NEB member of staff
- . **an** AIDS sufferers hostel

. Some acronyms may be considered as abbreviations. For example:

. **an** <u>URL</u> for the ⇒ Uniform Resource Locator ⇐ **an acronym**
  ⇑

pronounced as **earl** - it is preceded by **an**

. **a** <u>URL</u> for the ⇒ Uniform Resource Locator ⇐ **an abbreviation**
  ⇑

pronounced as a series of three letter as **'you-are-ell'**

. Aids or AIDS for the $\Rightarrow$ Acquired Immune Deficiency Syndrome)

There is some confusion about its classification. In some dictionaries, it is an abbreviation not an acronym. Furthermore, it has two versions of presentation (see above). However, **Aids** is more commonly used in the UK.

. <u>**acute**</u>

It means a serious disease, but it is commonly used to refer to something very serious, very intelligent or severe as illustrated below:
> . Due to political upheavals, there is **an acute shortage of basic food stuff** in Ukraine.
> . As a criminal psychologist, she is **an acute observer** of people she meets in all walks of life.
> . In this industry, <u>**competition for managerial jobs is acute**</u>.

it is very difficult to be successful due to severe competition↵
> . In winter, flu is <u>**an acute illness**</u>.

a serious disease but one which lasts only for a short time↵

See $\Rightarrow$ chronic

. <u>**acumen**</u>

It means the ability to think quickly, clearly and make good judgements. It is usually used to state a specific ability, such as:
. James shows great political acumen and he will stand for a parliamentary seat at the next General Election.
. Anne displayed considerable financial acumen at her first board meeting.

. <u>**AD (from Latin 'Anno Domini')**</u>

Anno Domini means 'in the year of our Lord.' In old writing, **AD** was written before the year, e.g.
> . This history book was published in AD 1875 in England.

The present day practice is to add AD to the year, e.g.
> . Bridlington Museum of Art was built in 1999 AD.

<u>**AD** indicates that the year is after Jesus Christ was believed to have been born. You do not add AD or BC (see BC) in day-to-day writing.</u>

See $\Rightarrow$BC and $\Rightarrow$**circa**

. ad hoc

It is from Latin. It means for a particular purpose only.
For instance:
- . Road traffic grew so much in our area that we had to form
  an ad hoc committee in order to raise this matter with our local
  government.
- . We can always arrange **an ad hoc** group meeting to deal with any
  future system's failure affecting our section.

. affect (and effect)

Some people are often confused when they want to use either **affect** or **effect**.
The word affect is a verb. It is an action verb which indicates some-
thing/someone has influenced or changed something/someone in some way:
For instance:
- . A new system will not affect our working hours.
- . Our company's declining sales will affect our annual bonus.
- . A heavy snow fall usually affects the sale of ice cream in the UK.

On the other hand, effect is a noun. See $\Rightarrow$ effect

. agnostic(and atheist)

Both words **agnostic** and **atheist** mean the same but there is an important
difference between their usage and the sense conveyed by them. (See atheist)

We use agnostic when we refer to someone who believes that it is impossible
to know whether God exists or not, e.g.
- . It was a lively debate between a Catholic believer and **an agnostic**.

See $\Rightarrow$ atheist

. alibi

It is from Latin and it means **elsewhere**. It should be used only when an
accused person has to prove that he/she was in another place at the time of a
crime and could not have committed the crime/offence. Some people use it to
mean an excuse for something they have done wrong, e.g.
- . The suspect had **an alibi** for the day when the murder was committed.
- . She thought her story would be taken as **an alibi** but the panel took it
  as an excuse for her not being able to come on time.

Its use for a simple excuse as illustrated by the last example should be avoided.

. all ready (already)

All ready and **already** do not mean the same. The use of **already** is illustrated under its own heading.

All ready is a phrase consisting of two separate words. It is used to express a variety of circumstances in order to indicate that a state or state of affairs is arranged, completed, organized, prepared and some other similar meanings. It is also used to imply that one or more people are agreeable, or ready to do something. For instance:
>   . They were **all ready** to board the coach when the coach arrived.
>   . We are **all ready** to sign this contract.
>   . Shops are **all ready** for the opening ceremony of a new precinct.

See ⇒ already

. all right

Write as two separate words - **all right. Alright** is not considered as a phrase in standard English, despite the fact that many people use it. It is substandard. All right means satisfactory, agree and other similar meanings, depending on the context in which it is being used. For example:
>   . **all** Is this seat all right, sir?
>   . How do you feel? All right.
>   . We played all right but we must improve our team performance.

. all together (and altogether)

All together and **altogether** sound similar but they have different meanings. Altogether is discussed under its own entry. All together means at the same time or in the same place. For instance:
. Some football hooligans were roaming our High Street **all together** until late last night.
. Can we please keep our belongings **all together** in this room?
>   wish to keep belongings in the same room ↵   See ⇒ altogether

. already

Already can be used to express different situations relating to time.

For instance:
- It can refer to a particular time in the past, e.g.
  - The last bus to Luton has **already** left this bus stop three minutes ago.
- it can signify a surprise as some event happened earlier than expected e.g.
  - Anne is **already** here. There is no need to arrange a taxi for her now.
- it can refer to a problematic situation, e.g.
  - It is already 23 hours and there is no sign of Susan yet.
  - Our car is **already** full. What do we do now as we can't leave this luggage behind? Shall we hire a taxi?

On the whole, **already** relates to time and an event or occurrence that has happened by the time in question, which may be the present time ⟹ **now**.

See ⟹ all ready

. allusion (to something/someone)

Sometimes people are confused by **'allusion'** and **'illusion'** because these words sound similar. In fact, these are two separate words and render different meanings. **Illusion** is discussed under its own heading. **Allusion** means an indirect reference to something or someone, e.g.
- John's remarks were seen as an allusion to his early retirement.
- Plewnia's writing is best interpreted as an allusion to her early life during communist rule in Poland.

See ⟹ illusion

. alternate(and alternative)

Sometimes, **alternate** and **alternative** cause confusion. These two words are used for expressing different circumstances. Alternative is discussed under its own heading.

Alternate is used to mean every other, every second, interchanging, to take turns, or to follow in turn, e.g.
- Our weather forecast is **for alternate snow and rain** on Christmas Day.
  - snow and rain taking turns⤶
- As London is rather far from here, I visit my mother **on alternate weekends**.

. My wife works on **alternate Saturdays**.
. We had to give a ten-minute talk to our class and some tutors on **alternate week**s.

See ⟹ alternative

. alternative

Traditionally, the alternative was used to state a choice among two things or possibilities in terms of one of two possibilities or things. The modern tendency is to offer a choice in terms of either one thing or others, e, g.

. The **alternatives** are to telephone, send a fax, or send a letter through the ordinary postal system.
. We have several **alternatives** which include to reduce prices, to offer a bigger discount, to attach a free gift to each saleable item or to offer two for the price of one.
. We had **no alternative** but to cancel our hotel booking.

. although

Although is a conjunction. It is used to show a contrast between the meanings of two clauses in a sentence. For instance:

. **Although** our firm has made some profit it can still be bankrupt.
. Jim is often rude to my members of staff, although he is kind in many ways.
. We left Heathrow Airport thirty minutes late, **although** we landed at Frankfurt Airport at the scheduled time.

When you are commenting on a statement, **although** acts as **but** or **however**. It is illustrated by these examples. Usually, **although** is used in writing. Its equivalent is **though** which is discussed under its own heading.

See ⟹though

. altogether

It is used to express several things as exemplified below:
. total number or amount, e.g.
    . It will cost you £145.98 altogether
    . How many guests arrived? **Altogether**, 51 guests were present at the seminar.
. it can be used to give a summary of some event which has happened, e.g.

. Our trip to France was rather costly, short lived in a chill winter,
           but food and entertainment were excellent. **Altogether** we really
           had a good time for three days.
. it can be used to mean completely, wholly or in every way, e.g.
      . We discussed the union's proposal for two hours, but we could not
        altogether agree with their suggestion.
      . I don't think you **altogether** agree with me. See ⟹ all together

. amiable (and amicable)

Amiable and amicable are adjectives, but they are used in different ways.
Amicable is discussed under its own heading. Amiable is used to say that
someone is friendly, likeable or agreeable. It places emphasis on friendliness
and goodwill. For instance:
      . When I met Kay, I found her very **amiable**.
      . Our new neighbours are **amiable**.
      . I met Antonia on a train between Budapest and Frankfurt. we
        were amiable travelling companions throughout our journey.

See ⟹ amicable

. amicable

Amicable is used to say that something is done in a friendly way without
much fuss or a quarrel. For instance:
      . They have reached **an amicable** agreement regarding their
        inherited property.
      . In this office, our members of staff have **an amicable**
        working relationship.
      . I am pleased to receive **an amicable** letter from my previous
        employers concerning my pension matter.

These examples illustrate that 'amicable' relates to agreements and relationships which point to friendliness.

See ⟹ amiable

. ampersand - &

Ampersand's symbol is **&**. It stands for **'and'**. Its use should be restricted to
business names, e.g.
      . Once I worked for A & B Booksellers in Charing Cross Road.

It may be used where space is limited. On the other hand, it is not recommended to shorten it to jut **'n'** as some take-away food shops do so, e.g.

    . fish **'n** chips only £2.10

. annex/annexe

    . **annex** is a verb. It means to possess a land, area or country especially by force, e.g.

    . Germany annexed Czechoslovakia in 1939.

    . **annexe** is a noun. It means an additional building or area, e.g.

       . Maths classes are held in Hopkins Annexe.

       . Our offices are in a new annexe which is just apposite the main college building on North Street.

It is also used to mean an additional section of a document, e.g.

       . All references to 'land ownership' are listed in chronological order in the annexe, pages 200-202.

It is rather a formal use.

. These two words are not interchangeable. However, often people use them incorrectly.

. any

Any can function as a determiner, pronoun and adverb. It has a special use in the following circumstances:

    . in negative questions when you want to say 'it does not matter much', e.g.

    . You can sit **any where** you wish.

It should be noted that **'some'** is used with positive sentences. See ⇒ some

    . it can be used after **if** or **whether** in order to refer to an amount or a number, e.g.

       . How many guests will come today, **if any**?

       . Whether we sell **any** or not depends on the weather. (as in the case of an umbrella retailer)

    . it can be used with singular countable nouns to mean one of a number of things, e.g.

       . Can I choose one of the these jackets? You can choose **any** jacket you like.

. anybody
See ⇒ anyone

. any longer

It means that something which existed or was once true, does not exist or is untrue now, e.g.

> . Mr Brown is **no longer** our managing director, as he passed
> away last week.
> . Pam **no longer** lives at that address.

Note that **any longer** is placed in mid position in the sentence, and no commas are needed before or after it. It is placed at the end of a negative sentence, e.g.

> . I have been here since 11 a.m. I can't wait **any longer**.

In fact, any longer is considered rather a formal expression. Its informal equivalent is **any more**. See below.

. any more

It has the same meaning as **any longer**, as discussed above. Often it is placed at the end of a negative sentence, e.g.

> . They are not in love **any more**. At last, she left him.
> . Why cannot you ride a horse **any more**?

You cannot replace **any** by **no** in this expression. It is incorrect to say:

> . Why cannot you ride a horse **no more**?

                       incorrect use⏎

. Sometimes **'any more'** is used as a quantifier (adverb)e.g.

> . She does not have **any more** of those books which I bought for her.
> . By the time we returned to England, we didn't have **any more** money.

. Sometimes it is written as 'one word', which is not recommended.

. anyone

It is a pronoun. Similarly **anybody** is also a pronoun. These two pronouns are interchangeable as both mean the same. The following discussion also relates to anybody. It has the following special usage:

> . in negative sentences, it means **an important person,** e.g.
>> . John wasn't **anyone/anybody** before he won his Parliamentary
>> Seat to become a Member of Parliament.
> . often it is used to mean any person, e.g.
>> . Did you see **anyone/anybody** sitting in the parked car?

. This job is so straight forward that **anyone/anybody** can do it
        without any training.

. These words cannot be placed before a negative verb. For instance:
    . **Anyone/anybody** who helps in the kitchen will not be asked to
      clean the dormitory.
it should be replaced by **no one** and re-written as shown below:
    . **No one** who helps in the kitchen will be asked to clean the dormitory.

.apprehend(and comprehend)

In the broad sense, apprehend and comprehend mean **to understand**, but
they render some specific meanings. The word comprehend is discussed under its own heading. Apprehend is used in the following circumstances:
        . to mean arrest or seize someone, e.g.
            . At last, the police have **apprehended** the mass murderer.
        . to understand or recognize something by intuition instead of a
          mental process. In this context, its use is considered as
          'old-fashioned', e.g.
            . She said, 'I apprehend the reasons for his refusal to
              co-operate in this matter.'
See $\Rightarrow$ comprehend

. as

'As' can be a **preposition, adverb** and **conjunction**, depending on how it is
functioning in a clause/sentence. It is used in formal written English. Its
equivalent is **'like'**, which is common in informal English.
        . When **as** is a **preposition**, it expresses two different meanings.
          The following examples illustrate these meanings:
            (1). At present, David is working **as a postman**.
    describing **the nature of the work** done by David ↵as $\Rightarrow$ **preposition**
            (2). My computer can function **as a fax machine**.
    describing a particular function performed ↵ as $\Rightarrow$ **preposition**

. When **as** is **an adverb**, it expresses two different meanings. The following
  examples illustrate these meanings:
            (3). My car is **as new as his car**.
comparing two equal/similar objects↵ - as $\Rightarrow$ **adverb**

(4) . My wife hasn't known you as long **as I have**.

comparing two situations in terms of time⤶ **as** ⇒ **adverb**

It means that I have known you longer than my wife has known you.
.Examples 3 and 4 illustrate that as enables us to compare two situations,
people, objects, etc.

. When **as** is **a conjunction**, it expresses different meanings, depending
on the context in which it is used. Here are some examples to demonstrate
the different meanings which can be expressed:

(5) . **As** I learn more grammar, my confidence in English grows.

⇑ **as** ⇒ **conjunction**

describing a situation while something else is happening
(i.e. confidence in English is growing)

(6) . Please leave this shop now **as** we are about to close.

describing a reason for doing something⤶ **as** ⇒ **conjunction**

(7) . The chairman said, 'As you already know, I am about to retire.'

(8) . As we have found out, you are a confidence trickster.

adding some new information⤶ **as** ⇒ **conjunction**

(9) . Run as fast as he might, he could not win the race.

⇑ **as** ⇒ **conjunction**

emphasizing that something is being true and what follows is also true. In
other words:

. **However how fast he ran, he couldn't win the race**.

true statement ⤶   another true statement⤶

Therefore: However how fast he ran = Run **as** fast **as** he might

. **at**

It is a preposition. It is a source of confusion to many people. Its actual meaning depends on its usage in a particular situation, as exemplified below:

. use it to say where someone/something exists or happens, e.g.

(1) . Our train arrived fifteen minutes late **at** Victoria Rail Station.

(2) . We were at home watching our last holiday video film.

(3) . The bus stop for the number 11 bus is just at that corner.

. use it to say when something happens, e.g.

(4) . I didn't know them at the time of their wedding.

. use it to say where someone works or studies, e.g.
  (5) . I used to work **at** Barclays Bank in London.
  (6) . Rebecca is reading Roman History **at** Cambridge
    (it means at Cambridge University)
. use it to express the distance away from a particular place, e.g.
  (7) . We were staying **at about** 200 metres from the airport.
. use it to say in the direction of someone/something, e.g.
  (8) . A young man pointed a knife **at me** and demanded that I hand
    over my wallet to him.
  (9) . Some hooligans threw an empty can **at my parked car**.
. use it to indicate the age of someone when he/she does
  something (important), e.g.
  (10) . I left home **at** the age of 16.
  (11) . I got married again **at** 70 because I was lonely.

. atheist(and agnostic)

The word agnostic has already been discussed earlier. An atheist is a person
who believes that there is no God. e.g.
  . He was born into a Christian family but he is an atheist.
See ⇒agnostic

. at this moment in time

This phrase/expression means **now, currently or at present**. Some people
consider its use as pompous and avoid it. No one can stop you using it, if you
think it fits your purpose. It is often used in business communication, e.g.

  . I regret to inform you that **at this moment in time** we are unable to
    despatch goods, as our credit control department is still waiting to
    hear from one of your referees.

. awake(and wake)

  . **awake** is an adjective and a verb   . **wake** is a noun and a verb

These words confuse many of us, when we want to use one of them correctly.

. **Awake** – **when it is used as a verb,** its meaning depends on the context
        in which it is being used. This is illustrated below:

. **awake** – it means to rouse, emerge from sleep, to become conscious or alert, e.g.

. We live in a seaside town, where birds **awake** me everyday early in the morning.

. I **awoke** to a day of brilliant sunshine. ⇐ **past tense**

. **awake** – it means to rouse feelings, provoke, stir up, or excite someone, e.g.

. His racist speech awoke nationalistic feelings amongst his young followers against minorities in the country.

See ⇒awake to something

. **Awake** – when it is used as an adjective, it means not asleep, alert, alive, conscious, watchful or attentive, e.g.

. When she arrived in the early hour of the morning from London, I was already **wide awake**. (it means fully awake)

. I was **awake** after the accident, but suffering from an acute pain.

still conscious⏎

Note that awake as an adjective is not used before a noun.

. **awake to something**

In this phrase **awake** is used as a phrasal verb. This phrase is used when you want to say someone should be aware of something and its likely effects, e.g.

. Are you sure you're really **awake to the financial commitments involved in this venture**?

. It took us some time **to awake to the harsh realities of life**.

. **wake**

See ⇒awake and see ⇒ wake

. **back up/backup**

. **back up** as two words is a **verb** - it means to support, assist, or help, e.g.

. Some shoppers tried to back up the policeman who confronted an armed robber in our shopping precinct.

. You are required **to backup** your claim for travelling expenses.

. **back up** - in information technology, it means to copy data, software, or information, e.g.

. We back up our accounting data on CD-ROM's every day.
. **backup (or back-up)** is a **noun**. It means support, help or
reinforcement, e.g.
. During last night's civil disturbances, our local police had
back up from the neighbouring police force.
reinforcements↵

. **backup (or back-up)** ⇒ noun
In information technology, it means files, documents or whatever
copies on some electronic media, usually for security purposes. e.g.
. Our backup data on CD-ROMs is up-dated daily.

. backward/backwards

. **Backward is an adjective.** Its meaning depends on the context in
which it is being used. It can be used only before a noun.
(1). It is used to indicate a movement towards the back, e.g.
. Doris kept running fast without **a backward glance** to see
who was just behind her and won the race.
(2). It can be used to show that someone/something is moving in
the direction which points to no progress being made, e.g.
. Despite the fact that we have two more salesmen, our
sales analysis reveals **a backward trend**.
(3). You can use it express that someone/something is behind,
less successful or less developed in comparison, e.g.
. Our area is economically a backward region.
. Some children from deprived backgrounds are **backward
learners** in my class.
. **Backwards is an adverb**
(1). It is used to mean a position or place towards the rear or
back. It means in the direction of a position or a place that
is behind, e.g.
. I bent over backwards to make our new neighbours
feel welcome.
. Please take a step backwards.
(2). Use it to say towards a worst state, e.g.
. We have come so far under these terrible weather conditions,
but turning back would be **a step backwards**.
. Yesterday the patient appeared to be out of danger, but today
he is **slipping backwards**.

(3) . It can mean in the opposite direction, e.g.
     . My travel to my place of birth can only be described as
      a journey **backwards** through time.

. barely(also hardly and scarcely)

Barely, hardly and scarcely are adverbs, which render negative meanings,
'almost no '. Some writers place another negative word before them. These
words should not be preceded by any negative word. For instance:
 . I **couldn't barely** introduce my topic when someone shouted abuse at me.

incorrect use↵
 . I could **barely** introduce my topic when someone shouted abuse at me.

 correct use↵
It implies a negative aspect because I had spoken **for only a short time**.

 . This patient can **barely walk** a few steps without a nurse.
        ⇑

It has a negative meaning in the sense that the patient can walk only
a few steps without assistance.

 . There is **hardly any milk** left in this jug.

almost empty jug ↵

   . **Hardly a day goes by without** her is thinking of her daughter.
she never forgets about her daughter↵
     . Do you know John Brown? I **scarcely** ever met him.

        implying not much or just↵ - negative meaning
    . It was **scarcely** a happy visit, as we arrived at their home they had a
       ⇑   serious fire in their kitchen.
   implying **not** happy - negative meaning

. BC ('Before Christ')

It is used with dates which occurred before Jesus Christ was believed to have
been born, e.g.
  . Aristotle **(384-322 BC)** was a Greek philosopher.

See ⇒AD and ⇒**circa**

. <u>beside and besides</u>

The difference between **beside** and **besides** is not due to their spellings but their meanings. Furthermore, **beside** is a preposition and **besides** is a preposition as well as an adverb.

. <u>The preposition beside means next to someone/something,</u> e.g.

> . Anne, my wife, is sitting **beside a lady** wearing a red blouse.
>
> . There aren't many seats available, but you can sit **beside** me.

. <u>When besides functions as a preposition, it means in addition to someone/something,</u> e.g.

> . Which other major cities have you visited **besides** London?
>
> . Who else do you know here **besides** myself? No one. What a pity!

. <u>When besides functions as an adverb, it is used to add some additional information or remarks to what someone already has said,</u> e.g.

> . That restaurant is very expensive. **Besides**, it has rather small portions(of food).
>
> . That property needed costly renovation. **Besides,** it has no garage or even a driveway for our car.

These two examples illustrate that the **adverb besides** is not used on its own. It is followed by a comment on what you have just said in the previous part of the speech/writing.

. <u>between(--- ---me/I)</u>

The word **between** is a preposition as well as an adverb. 'me' and 'I' are personal pronouns (see ⟹ pronouns). **Between** can be used in different ways. For instance, it is commonly used to indicate a relationship or connection. Since the preposition **between** is followed by an **object**, the correct pronoun after **between** is me (objective pronoun), e.g.

> . Between you and **me**, I think they are penniless, and ashamed to ask us for some money.
>
> . Between you and **I**, she is going to resign from her post.

> grammatically incorrect ↵

> **But:**   . **I** do know him well.

It is grammatically correct usage because **I** is a subjective personal pronoun.

. bloc/block

These words can be a source of confusion. **Bloc** is a noun, but **block** can function as a noun as well as a verb. These words mean different things. The word **bloc** means a group of some countries, parties or people joined together because they share similar interests. For instance
. Soviet Bloc . Eastern Bloc . Non-aligned Movement bloc . Western Bloc

On the other hand, '**block**' can be used in a variety of ways to express a wide rang of meaning, e.g.
. This area of London is full of new **office blocks**.

tall office buildings↵
. There is a big **block** of stone.

a piece of stone that is square in shape ↵
. **As a verb it is used to indicate a variety of meanings,** e.g.
. Due to a serious car accident, all major roads in this area are
still **blocked**. (traffic cannot move as roads are full of vehicles)
For more meanings of '**block**' consult a quality dictionary.

.bona fide

This phrase is from Latin. It means real, genuine, authentic, not false. It is used before a noun, e.g.
. I believe that Johan gave us a **bona fide reason** for his late arrival.
. This is a **bona fide** certificate of a new employee's teacher
training qualification.

. bottom line (or the bottom line)

This phrase has its origin in the accountancy field, where it means the profit or loss figure after taking into account all necessary calculations. It is also commonly used to refer to the most important consideration when making a decision. It can also mean the lowest price one can accept. The following examples illustrate these meanings:
. The **bottom line for** 2004 was a net profit of 12 million.
. The **bottom line of** our decision is to sell our house as this offer
of purchase is the highest we have received.
. What is the bottom line you can accept for this car?
My **bottom line** is £12 000.

. bottom out

This is a phrasal verb/expression. It is used to refer to an unfortunate circumstance, situation or condition which is no longer getting worse, e.g.
. Our sales analysis has revealed that low winter sales are bottoming out.
. The price war between major electrical consumer goods stores is showing signs of bottoming out.

. breakdown/break down

. **breakdown** - one word is a noun
. **break down** - two words is a phrasal verb/phrase

. The noun breakdown has a wide range of meanings, e.g.
. She has just recovered from her **breakdown**.
. **The breakdown of our marriage** is the biggest disaster in my life.
. This car price includes our free 24-hour **breakdown** recovery service anywhere in the country for one year.

In the last example, **breakdown** means a car failure or some kind of malfunction. It can be used for all kinds of vehicle or machine failures, or malfunctioning. Here are some more examples:
. At this stage, we were not expecting the **breakdown of our sales** negotiations.
. This will lead to **the break down of law** and order in this town.
. **The breakdown of food** in our digestive system is essential for our health and survival.

. The verb break down also has a wide range of meanings, e.g.
. Our car was **broken down** on the motorway on that rainy night.
. When she received this terrible news, she **broke down** and screamed.
                     lost her emotional control↲
. Due to late night shift work during the whole last year, her health **broke down**. (health became bad)

. breath/breathe

. **breath** is a noun   . **breathe** is a verb

. The noun breath has a wide range of meanings.

Its most common usage refers to the air that we take into our lungs and send out through the mouth or nose for our survival. For instance:
. I had to stop **for breath** several times before I could reach

the top floor of London Post Office Tower.

. If you eat garlic regularly in the UK, you may be labelled as having bad **breath**. (bad smell from the mouth)

uncountable noun here ↵

. Please take a deep **breath**.

as much breath that can enter the lungs at one time↵ -countable noun here

. It can also mean slight evidence of something, e.g.

. A breath of suspicion is sufficient for Scotland Yard to launch an inquiry into a murder case.

. The verb breathe can express a variety of situations as exemplified below:

. In that part of the world, the air was so cold I could hardly **breathe**.

difficult to take air into my lungs and send it out through my mouth or nose ↵

. Please **don't breathe** smoke in my office, as it is making me sick.

⇑

to produce smoke from the mouth or nose and spread it in the office

. This high quality pair of shoes is rather expensive but it allows my **feet to breathe**. (implies that the air can circulate or move through them)

. breathe

See ⇒breath

. broach/brooch

. broach is a verb   **. brooch** is a noun

These words confuse some writers, because they sound similar. They are not related words and have different meanings and usage as outlined below.

. broach means to talk about something that is difficult to discuss because some people either do not agree about it or find it rather embarrassing, e.g.

. I do not like **to broach the subject of religion** at my workplace.

. At our home, we were not allowed to broach the subject of sex with anybody.

. brooch is a piece of jewellery which has a pin at its back, so that it can pinned to a blouse, etc. for instance:

. My grandmother often fastens an attractive brooch to her top clothes.

. brooch

See ⟹broach/brooch

. calendar/calender

These words are often a source of confusion because of their spellings and pronunciation.
   . calendar(noun) – it is a kind of chart which shows days, weeks and
                      months of a year.
   . calender (noun) - it is a machine used in the printing/paper industry
                      for pressing paper or cloth...

. can (and may)

Can and **may** are modal auxiliary verbs. Their past tense forms are **could** and **might** respectively. These words are used in a variety of ways to indicate different situations. However, in one sense they share the same meaning which is **to be allowed, permitted or ask for permission**.

. The modal verb **can** is used for less formal situations for asking for permission, giving or refusing permission than the modal verb **may**. Its use suggests rather relaxed circumstance. This is exemplified below:
   . It is getting late to get home. **Can** I leave you now? (for permission)
   . Yes, you **can** do so. (permission given)
   . You **can't** stay up late tonight. (permission not given)
. The modal verb 'can' can also be used to express some other meanings, e.g.
   . I **can** come back tomorrow. (indicating someone to do)
   . It **can** rain at any time. (pointing to the possibility of rain happening)
   . You **can** hire a taxi, if it is too far for you to walk. (suggestion/advice)
   . Anne is very good at languages, as she **can** speak German.
   expressing Anne's ability to do something ↵ - speak German

. cannon/canon

These words have different meanings but often cause some confusion to many writers. **Cannon** functions as a noun and verb. **The noun cannon** refers to a large gun made of metal, which was used to fire metal or stone balls. In these days, it is rather an old-fashioned weapon, as there are other types of armament. Nowadays, there are also some other types of cannons such as a **water cannon**. A water cannon is a machine that produces a power-ful water flow. Water cannons are used by the police in order to control dem-onstrators.

<u>**The verb cannon**</u> means to hit, or to collide with something or somebody with a great force, e.g.

. He lost control of his car, **cannoning into** a tree and was killed instantly.

<u>**The other noun canon**</u> - it is, in the first place, connected with the church:

    . It can be a title of a clergyman.

    . It is a rule or a standard laid down by the church to regulate religious or moral practices.

. <u>**It has some other meanings which include:**</u>

    . a list of books or other works of an author that are accepted as authentic and important, e.g. **the Kipling canon**.

. <u>cannot/ can not/ can't</u>

The word cannot is an auxiliary verb. It is used to express inability or with-holding permission, e.g.

    . We **cannot** travel tonight by air to Japan.   (expressing incapacity)

    . The captain says 'passengers **cannot disembark** from the plane yet.'

. <u>cannot = cannot = can't (contracted form)</u>

. Some writers make a distinction between **cannot** and **can not**. They restrict the use of **can not** for emphasis only, e.g.

    . You **can not** borrow my car this morning.

This distinction is not widely recognised. Its contracted form **can't** is generally used in speech and informal writing.

. <u>canon</u>

See ⇒cannon

. <u>canvas/canvass</u>

<u>canvas</u> - it is used as a noun. It is a strong rough fabric for making tents, etc. The word <u>canvass</u> is a verb which means to ask somebody to support a particular person or a political party. It is particularly used when a politician or his/her supporters solicit votes for the politician and/or his/her political party. It can also be used to find out people's opinions about any matter concerning a particular community or locality. For instance:

. I have been very busy this week **canvassing residents** in this area
  for their views on the proposed closure of our hospital.
. A number of party workers from several political parties have
  called us tonight **canvassing for votes**.

. <u>capacity for...</u>

This should be used to say something about someone's <u>**inborn ability**</u> <u>**not**</u>
<u>**learnt skills**</u>.
    . His **capacity for** speaking and writing in five languages amazed me.
    . Our youngest son has an enormous capacity for working hard.

. <u>censor/censure</u>
        . <u>censor</u> - it is both a noun and a verb.
        . <u>censure</u> - it is also both a noun and a verb.

These words confuse many writers. **<u>The noun censor</u>** means a person who is
authorised to examine publications such as books, films, letters, etc., in order
to suppress partly or wholly any information unacceptable to the authority.

    . <u>**The verb censor**</u> means to examine the publications in various
      formats in order to remove partially or wholly unacceptable
      information, e.g.
    . All letters from Russia are censored in Moscow before they leave
        Russia for their destinations across the world.
    . News reports from the war zones in Iraq were heavily censored by
      the broadcasting authorities for political reasons.

. <u>**The noun censure**</u> – it means strong blame or criticism.
        . The next Parliamentary Election will be a vote of censure on
          the current government.
. <u>**The verb censure**</u> – it means to blame or criticize harshly, e.g.
        . He was censured by his employers for leaking sales data to
          another company.
. <u>chronic</u>

Firstly, it refers to a serious disease which is slow to develop but lasts for a
long time. Secondly, it is also used to mean something very serious or very
bad which exists for a long time. In informal English, it means very bad, e.g.
    . We had **chronic shortage of sugar** some years ago.
    . In some countries, many people suffer from **chronic asthma**.

. Our team effort was so **chronic** that we lost the game. (informal English)

. **circa (from Latin)**

It is abbreviated by a small **c**. It is used with dates in order to indicate
'about' when dates are uncertain e.g.
   . Buddha (the enlightened) (c.563 – c.483 BC)
   According to tradition, he achieved enlightenment when sitting beneath
   a banyan tree near Buddh Gaya in Bihar, India.

See ⇒AD and ⇒**BC**

. **collaborate/cooperate** The word <u>collaborate</u> a verb. It has two specific
meanings:

   1 . <u>to work together towards the achievement of some common goal,</u> e.g.
      . A group of community workers and some police officers will
      collaborate on this new community project for young people.
   2. <u>to work together with the enemy of one's own country as a traitor, e.g.</u>
      . Some spies from the West **collaborated with** the KGB (state secret
      police) of USSR during the Cold War.

   . **cooperate** – <u>it is also a verb and has almost the same meaning as</u> the
                <u>first meaning of the verb collaborate,</u> e.g.
         . My country will **cooperate** with your country in
            order to develop trade between our two countries.
   . **cooperate** <u>also means to assist or help willingly,</u> e.g.
            . Anne always **cooperates with** me whenever
            she thinks I have too much work to do.

. These examples illustrate that the verbs **collaborate** and **cooperate** are
not always interchangeable. They do have similar meanings but they
also differ in some respects.

. **comparatively/relatively**

Both **comparatively** and **relatively** are adverbs. These words are used for a
comparison with somebody or something else. The comparison shows how
much or how far somebody or something matches, or equals somebody or
something. Thus, a comparison is made in relation to a standard. it is, therefore, advisable that one should avoid using these words without a comparison. For instance:

. Anne is **comparatively** taller than Margaret.

. We made a loss this year but it is relatively small when compared with the losses of the last two years.

          . Mark is **comparatively** intelligent.

     is comparison intended?⏎

If it is so, in relation to whom? It is better to say more, less, fairly, very or reasonably, e.g.   . Mark is **very** intelligent.

.comprehend

It is already mentioned under apprehend (see apprehend). Like apprehend, it means to understand something through the mental process instead of intuition. It is used to emphasize that something is difficult to grasp or understand, e.g.   . The chemical process described in the lecture was beyond me

          to comprehend.

          it means that the lecture was **too difficult for me to understand**.

                 negative sense ⏎

See ⟹ apprehend

.confidant/confident

   . **confidant (also confidante)** – it is a noun. It means someone you confide in - that is to tell someone your secrets or give personal information entrusting that person will not disclose it to other people, e.g.

       . I do not have any trusted confidant.

       . One expects that both husband and wife are close confidants of one another/each other.

Since it is derived from **French**, confidante is used for a female.

   . **confident** - it is an adjective meaning sure of oneself, e.g.

       . Today she appears to be more relaxed and **confident**.

       . Almost all my students feel **confident of** passing this subject.

. conform to/with

The use of a correct preposition after the verb **conform** can be a cause of confusion. It has a number of usages as illustrated below:

     . **conform to** - to observe some rules, obey some rules and regulations

or accept and act according to a set of norms, e.g.
. All employees are expected to conform to this company's
rules and regulations as described in the handbook.

. **conform with** - it is used to mean 'agree with', or 'match something
with some other thing'. Its usage is less specific than
the use of **conform to**, e.g.
. The health inspector reported that our hotel kitchen did
not **conform with** safety standards.

. connection between/with
. **connection** is a noun. Its less common spelling is **connexion**.
. **between** and **with** are prepositions

Either of these prepositions can come after **connection**. Sometimes it is rather puzzling when deciding which of these prepositions should come after
connection. The following illustrations exemplify their correct usage:
. **connection between** – it means a link or relationship between two
things, ideas, people, etc., e.g.
. There is a direct **connection between** poor health and poverty.
. **connection with** – it means a link with something, e.g.
. His sudden departure seems to have some **connection** with the
telephone call he received just before he left.

. consensus

It is a singular uncountable noun. It means a general opinion or an agreement
about something, e.g.
. There was a **consensus** about the effects of job cuts.
. There was a **general** consensus about the effects of job cuts.
. The **consensus is** that John will represent us at the conference.
need to add of opinion⏎

. consequent/consequential

These words are adjectives and cause some confusion when someone is deciding which one to use to mean ' **a result or as a result**'.
. **consequent** - it means something is happening **'as a direct
result'** The emphasis is on **'direct'**, e.g.
. If I do not go to work today, there will be a

consequent loss of earnings.

loss of earnings ⏎ - as a direct result of not working

. **consequential** - it has two distinct meanings as illustrated:
      (1) . it is used mainly in formal and legal contexts to
          mean something is happening **'as an indirect**
          result or **effect'**, e.g.
            . The Royal Mail has lost our parcel. we can make a
            claim for **the consequent loss** - the cost of
            goods lost and postage paid. We can also claim
            for **the consequential loss of profit**, which we
            would have made if they had delivered the parcel.
      (2) . it means significant or important, e.g.
            . Our report includes a number of relevant
            consequential issues which were outside the
            remit of this enquiry.

See also ⟹ subsequent

. **cooperate**

See ⟹ collaborate/cooperate

. **dare**

It is both a verb and a noun. It can be either an ordinary verb or a modal verb.
It is rather an unusual verb and requires some explanation. It can be used to
express:
    (1) . when you want to say that someone has the courage to do
        something or should not be afraid to do something, e.g.
          . Jackie did not **dare to** walk out of the conference although
            she found it extremely boring.
          . I do not **dare to** see the dying person.

These examples also show that **dare** can function like any ordinary verb,
when it is followed by a **'to' infinitive**.

    (2) . when it is used as a modal verb, it is not followed by a 'to'
        infinitive clause, e.g.
          . Nobody **dare** walk alone along the east bank of this river.
          . Kay dares not report the whole matter.

. How **dare** she conceal the information?

In these two examples **dare** is followed by the **base form of the verb**, without **'to' infinitive**, but the meaning is the same as when it is followed by **to**. **'Dare'** is used as a **modal verb** only in negative sentences and questions as illustrated above. It is not used in the progressive sentences. The use of dare does not mean to say that an event or action really occurred. See ⟹ need

. data/datum

. **datum** – singular noun   and   . **data** – plural form of datum
In the age of information technology, data is treated as a **collective singular noun**, e.g.
. The **data was** extracted from 2000 forms completed by respondents.
. The data **has** to be processed to become useful information.
. This is sales data.

. deadly/deathly

Both words refer to death but in some different ways.
. **deadly** – adjective and adverb   and   . **deathly** – adjective and adverb
These words have different meanings as illustrated below.

. **deadly** – when it is used as **an adjective**, it means something **can kill,** e.g.
     . He has a **deadly knife** in his hand.
     . He was given a **deadly poison** to drink by his business enemies.
.**deadly** – when it is used as **an adverb**, it implies as if someone is dead,
   e.g.
     . When we met her at that bus stop, she was **deadly** cold.

. It is also used in informal English (spoken) to mean extremely, e.g.

     . I am deadly serious about this car.

.**deathly** – when it is used as **an adverb**, it means resembling death, or like a dead person e.g.
     . Mark was deathly pale with fear and trembling.
     . We were all deathly still and waiting for the next announcement.

.**deathly** – when it is used as **an adjective**, it means extreme, or intense e.g.

. As he began his lecture, a <u>**deathly silence**</u> descended in the hall.

. When we arrived late in the night, there was a **deathly quiet** in our street.

. <u>debatable(and questionable)</u>

. <u>**debatable**</u> – it is an adjective <u>and</u>   . **questionable** – it is also an adjective
These two words have different meanings but sometimes people want to be tactful and use debatable instead of questionable. The use of **debatable** is correct when some people have different opinions about something and want to discuss these openly, e.g.

>   . It is **debatable** whether the launch of this new product will improve our profit within the next six months.

>   . Indeed, your suggestion contains a number of **debatable** points.

See ⟹ questionable

. <u>defective/deficient</u>

Both words are adjectives. They have related meanings but not exactly the same meaning.

>   . <u>**defective**</u> <u>– it is used to mean something is faulty, something that does not operate properly or satisfactorily,</u> e.g.

>>   . Our printer seems to be **defective** as it keeps jamming up.

>>   . We can offer you 50 % discount on these goods because they are slightly **defective**.

>   . <u>**deficient**</u> <u>– it means someone or something is lacking in something, which is an essential part of someone or something,</u> e.g.

>>   . My doctor told me that my regular food was **deficient** in vitamin A.

>>   . His bowling techniques are unique but he is **deficient** in physical strength for the fast bowling.

. <u>Note that these words are **interchangeable only** when they are used to refer to human senses,</u> e.g.

>>   . My grandmother's left eye is **deficient/defective** because she is now 96 years old.

.<u>deficient</u>
See ⟹ defective/deficient

. <u>despatch/dispatch</u>

These two words have the same meaning because despatch and dispatch are alternative spellings. It is both a noun and a verb and their usage is illustrated below:

. **dispatch** – when it is used as a noun it means an act of sending something or someone somewhere, e.g.
   . Your goods will be ready for our **despatch/dispatch** car within ten minutes.
   . My grandfather's name was mentioned in several **dispatches** sent from the Western Front in the First World War.
. **dispatch** – when it is used as a verb it means to send something somewhere or to someone, e.g.
   . Your goods were **despatched/dispatched** yesterday to India by air mail.
   . The Defence Minister just announced, 'Foreign Legion troops are ready **to be despatched/dispatched** to the war torn area..'

. **despite**

It is a preposition and used mainly with a noun or gerund to mean that something is true or happened, e.g.
   . **Despite** the gale force winds last night, I still went out for a stroll as usual after my evening meal.
   . **Despite facing** some financial difficulties, he still sends me flowers.
     gerund ↵

. Note that it will be wrong to say/write: despite of facing---. The preposition despite stands alone. Therefore, there is no such phrase as **despite of.**

The equivalent of despite is in spite of see ⇒ in spite of

. **disinterested/uninterested**

Both words are adjectives and have different meanings. Sometimes people use them interchangeably without knowing the precise meanings of these words.

. **disinterested** - the following examples illustrate its correct usage:
   . Our solicitor gave us **disinterested advice** regarding this dispute.
   . The chairman of the Inquiry was **disinterested** in both parties' pleas.

These examples illustrate that **disinterested** means not to get involved emotionally in order to remain impartial, unbiased or fair in listening to some sort of dispute, judging matters or giving advice.

. The word **disinterested** is also used in spoken English in place of
   uninterested (disinterested = uninterested) which is not recommended, as
   it is considered incorrect use.
   . **uninterested** - it means you do not want to know someone or
      something, e.g.
         . I am **uninterested** in ball games.
         . She is **uninterested** in reading books.
If you compare these two examples with the other two examples under disinterested, you can see that uninterested is used in different contexts. For this reason, it is incorrect to use these two words interchangeably.

. doubtful/dubious

Doubtful and **dubious** are adjectives. They can be used interchangeably in some contexts. Why cannot we use them interchangeably in all contexts? The reason is that **dubious** has two specific meanings. One of these meanings is not shared by **doubtful**. Their meanings and usage are illustrated below:

   . **doubtful and dubious** - both mean not sure or certain about something
     or about doing something, e.g.
   . She is **doubtful/dubious about** the idea of moving to London for a job.
   . It is **doubtful/dubious** whether this year our sales revenue will be as
     much as it was last year.
     Both doubtful and dubious can be followed by **if, that** or **whether,** e.g.
   . We are **doubtful/ dubious that/if/whether** John will win this year's
     Milk Race.

   . **dubious** is also used to mean probably **dishonest** or bad, e.g.
   . It appears that he is involved in some **dubious** business dealings.
   . I do not wish to take part in this plan as in my view it is of a
     dubious nature. (bad/ dishonest)

. each

It is a pronoun. It means every one of two or more people or things. It can cause some confusion about the correct use of a verb before and after it. The following examples demonstrate the correct form of a verb with each:

. When it is before a singular noun, it is followed by a
   singular verb, e.g.
         . **Each** member **has been invited** for tonight's celebration.
         . **Each** of us **is happy** to be here to welcome you home.

refers to one person↵ ⇒singular noun
         . **Each one** of these football players of this club is very rich.

it is always singular↵ and thus the verb form is also singular

. When it comes after a plural noun, it is followed by the plural form
   of the verb, e.g.
         . My wife and I each **have** some very old picture postcards.
         . They **each have held** beautiful bouquets of roses in their hands.

 In these days, the social norm is to avoid using sexist language and attitudes.
Before the avoidance of exist language usage, the rule was to **use a male
pronoun**, when referring to a group of male and female students, male and
female members of a club and other such groups. It is now acceptable practice to use **his/her** or **they** in place of the male pronoun. For instance:
         . Each student contributed towards the restoration of
           the local church in accordance with **his/ her** wish.
         . Each member is associated with **their** local branch.
                      in place of his/her ↵
In fact, some people do not like the idea of using **a plural pronoun** with
each because it is grammatically incorrect. If you do not feel comfortable
with either his/her or their, it is best to re-construct the sentence with out
each, e.g.
         . All members are associated with their local branches.

. each other/one another

Strictly speaking, in accordance with the old rule of grammar, **each other**
and **one another** pronouns are not interchangeable. The old rule restricted
the use of **each other** to mean two persons only. On the other hand, **one another** should be used to refer to more than two people.

The modern tendency is to disobey the old rule and thus use these pronouns
interchangeably. For instance:
   . My brother and I can wear **each other's** jackets.

Note that the possessive form is **each other's not** ⇒ each others'

. In my family, we all care very much for <u>**one another**</u>.

        several persons are involved↵ **- old rule applied**

. In my family, we all care very much for <u>**one another/each other**</u>.

        several persons are involved↵ **- old rule disobeyed**

. **effect (and affect)**

The word **effect** is a noun as opposed to '**affect**' which is a verb (see affect). It means the result, consequence or influence of something/someone on something/someone:

    . A large number of people believe that television has **an adverse effect** on children's behaviour.

    . Most drugs have some **side effects**.

See ⇒ affect

. **e.g.**

It is an abbreviation of the Latin phrase - **exempli gratia**. It means for example as used in this chapter frequently. It has two full stops and a comma is placed before it. Some people write it without full stops. The placing of full stops is recommended, as you will find this practice in some quality dictionaries and other grammar books.

. **either**

It is a common word, which can function as a determiner, pronoun and adverb. It can cause some confusion. In essence, it means **one or the other of two**. Its usage is exemplified below:

    . <u>when either is functioning as a pronoun or determiner,</u> e.g.

      . You can sit on **either side of these two rows of seats**.

      . We could not park our car on **either side** of your street.

      . There are two categories of tomatoes which are A and B. I can supply you with **either of these** immediately.

        . **Either** category <u>is</u> acceptable.

    either takes a singular verb↵

<u>These examples show that **either** should be used to refer to things or people to mean one or the other of two.</u>

    . <u>when either is functioning as an adverb,</u> e.g.

. Our bus did not arrive on time and the underground trains
were not operating **either**.

. The above example demonstrates that **either** can be used to support a
negative statement by way of stating another similar situation.

. We knew your plan of action. It was not a secret, <u>either</u>.
. They did not reply to our letter immediately.
We did not reply **either**.

. These two examples explain that **either** is used to add further information
to a statement.

. either --- or---

It is a coordinating conjunction used to emphasise a choice, e.g.

. **Either** <u>you go to see these clients today</u>, **or** <u>I will see them myself today</u>.

choice 1 ↵   choice 2 ↵

. At the next roundabout, you can turn **either** right **or** left.
. When you are linking clauses by using this coordinating conjunction, you
can replace <u>or</u> with <u>or else</u>, e.g.
. If you want to come with me tomorrow, **either** you finish this job,
now <u>or else</u> ask Jackie to do it for you in your absence.

instead of **or**↵

. When should you use a singular or a plural verb with this coordinating conjunction?

. when both parts of the construction are 'singular', a singular
verb should be used, e.g.

. Either Anne or John **has arrived**.
. Either a student or a member of staff <u>is</u> permitted free of
charge tonight.

. when both parts of the construction are 'plural', a plural verb
should be used, e.g.

. Either security guards or police officers **were wearing**
blue uniforms.

. when one part of the construction is 'singular', and the other part is
'plural', verb agrees with the subject that is next to it, e.g.

. Either some directors or the financial **director has decided** to
give all members of staff an annual bonus.

See ⟹ neither--- nor---

. et al.

It is from a Latin phrase **et alii/alia**, meaning **'and others'**. This abbreviation is used in the listing of names or whatever to indicate that there are more of the same, e.g.

> . She travelled to Japan, India, China, Australia, **et el**.
> . Antonia wrote 'History of Budapest', 'A Train Journey
> from Budapest to Frankfurt', 'My Homeland', **et.al**.

In fact, it is usually used in formal writing. It ends with a full stop.

. etc.

It is an abbreviation derived from the Latin phrase **et cetera** (or **etcetera**). It is used at the end of a list to state that other items of the same type or class and other things or persons should be included or could have been mentioned e.g.

> . Robin Hood, Jon Baker, Joan Clarke, Colin Smith, etc.

. even though

See ⇒ though

. everybody/everyone

Everybody and **everyone** are both pronouns. They both mean every person. They can be used interchangeably, e.g.

> . **Everybody/everyone** will be allowed to take part. (stress on every)
> . In our class **everyone/everybody** contributed towards the maths
> teacher's retirement present.

. Note that everybody and everyone take singular verbs.

. When '**everyone**' is written as two words '**every one**', it means each person or thing in a group. It is used to place emphasis on each individual person or thing, e.g.

> . Police will interview **every one** who lives in this area.(stress on one)

. facetious

It is an adjective. It means not serious, humorous or flippant. It is used to indicate that someone should not behave humorously, when it would be better to be serious, e.g.

> . Everybody is gravely concerned about the sad news. You should
> not make facetious remarks.

. Two students in my class are rather facetious and do not take their assignments seriously.

. facility

It is a noun that is used in the following ways:
- . to refer to someone's natural ability to learn something , his/her skill or ease of doing something, e.g.
  - . Anne has a remarkable **facility for writing speeches**. (skill)
  - . We were talking about your great **facility for languages**.
    natural born ability/talent⏎
- . it is used in its plural form **facilities** to refer to something that is for a particular purpose, e.g.
  - . You are welcome to use our sports facilities .
  - . Office premises are required to have **facilities for disabled staff**.
  - . Alongside an insurance service, we also provide **bank facilities**.   (banking service)
- . it can be used in its **singular form to mean a specific feature** of something that enables you to do some additional things, e.g.
  - . At the checkout, you can pay by credit card for your shopping and use our new **cash withdrawal facility**.
  - . This calculator includes a facility for storing information.
- . **There is no need to overuse 'facility.** For instance:
  - . We offer colour photocopying facilities.
  - . We can photocopy in colour.

The last example is clearer and simple.

. factitious

It is an adjective. It means untrue, unreal or not genuine. it is used when something is deliberately contrived for an ulterior motive*, e.g.
- . The current demand for petrol is factitious because of the rumour that the oil producing countries are about to cut oil production drastically.

A similar word is **fictitious** which is discussed under its own heading.

* contrived for an **ulterior motives** means ⟹ hidden motives

See ⟹ fictitious

. farther/ further/farthest/furthest

These words are not interchangeable in all contexts because **further** has some additional meanings. When referring to a physical distance, you can use these words interchangeably e.g.

. It is **farther/further** to Moscow from London than it is to Paris.

. We already have walked **farther/further** than we planned.

. Archway is the **farthest/furthest** district of London from this area.

. Further can also be used to mean additional or more, e.g.

. I would like to ask you **a further question**.

. I think they will need **further** time to finish this job.

. Are there any **further** questions?

. Further can also be used as a verb, meaning to help towards the development of something, e.g.

. I believe this employment will **further** my skills and experience.

. We must work together **to further** the cause of freedom and democracy in our country.

. farthest

See ⟹ farther/ further/farthest/furthest

. fatal/fateful

These words relate to events that have decisive or momentous consequences, but they are used in very different contexts to express dissimilar meanings.

. **fatal** – it is an adjective, meaning causing death. It can also mean some thing that can cause disease, failure, disaster or a tragic consequence, e.g.

. Every year, several thousands of people are involved in **fatal road accidents**.

. At this stage, stopping production will be **a fatal mistake**.

causing a failure of great magnitude.↵

See ⟹lethal as it also pertains to death

. **fateful** – it is also an adjective, which usually comes before a noun. It is used to refer to an important event that has some serious and conclusive effects on some future events, e.g.

. Often I looked back to that **fateful day** in Paris ten years ago, when I met my future wife.

. fateful

See ⟹ fatal/fateful

. **female**

See ⇒gender/sex

. **fictitious**

It is an adjective. It means untrue, imaginary or invented by someone, e.g.
  . I like your **fictitious characters** in this essay.
In essence, Like factitious, it also means untrue but both words render very

different meanings. See ⇒ factitious

. **forbear/forebear**
  . **forbear** – It can function as a noun and as a verb. When it is used as
   a noun, it can be spelled as **forebear**. As a noun it means ancestors, e.g.
      . One of my **forbears** was awarded the Victoria Cross in 1912
       for his outstanding bravery.
  . **forebear** – it functions as a noun only. **Forebear** is equivalent in
   meaning to **forbear**, when the word forbear is functioning as a noun.
   Thus in the capacity of a noun, these two words are interchangeable, e.g.
      . His **forbears/forebears** were from Norway.
. The word forbear as a verb is used to say that you should hold back, or
  refrain from doing something or saying something, e.g.
      . At a time like this, you should **forbear** from making any
       defamatory remarks.
      . Please **forbear** from interrupting each speaker until you are
       invited by the speaker to ask questions.

. **former**
See ⇒ latter/former

. **further**
See ⇒ farther/ further/farthest/furthest

. **furthest**
See ⇒ farther/ further/farthest/furthest

. **gender/sex**

The word gender is a noun, meaning male or female. Similarly, sex is also a
noun and means the same as gender. It has another obvious meaning.

Both words refer to the same two groups into which people, animals and plants are classified. In grammar, by gender we mean **masculine (male)** and **feminine (female)** that are different in gender, e.g.

. host ⇒masculine noun /male . hostess ⇒ feminine noun /female

. **When is it preferable to use gender or sex ?** This is exemplified below:
  . Sometimes **sex** can have a double meaning or its use is not suitable or prudish. In such circumstances, it is advisable to use **gender,** e.g.
    . Recently, a young woman applied to become a football referee but because of **her gender**, she was not successful in getting a job in a male dominated sport.
    . Indeed, sometimes, I like being in the company of the **opposite gender**.
  . Sometimes it is better to avoid using gender or sex. If so, use male or female, e.g.
    . Both male and female candidates are equally qualified to apply for this post.

  . In the UK, for some legal requirements in order to identify male and female, the word sex is used, e.g.
    . Please tick an appropriate box: **Sex**   male   female

  . Prospective members of either sex can apply for the membership.

. **gourmand/gourmet/glutton**

These three words refer to food and thus it is easy to misuse them. Both gourmand and glutton are similar in meaning, but all three do not mean quite the same as illustrated below:
  . **gourmand** - it is a noun, meaning someone who eats too much food, as he/she enjoys it very much. It is used for someone whose eating habits you disapprove of. It is an insult to call someone a gourmand, e.g.
    . He is a **gourmand** whom you can find tucking into huge portions in junk food restaurants.
  . **glutton** – a noun. It has the same meaning as gourmand and is also used in disapproving way as an insult to the person(s), e.g.
    . Some gluttons at that table are **stuffing** themselves.(eating too much)
  . **gourmet** – as a noun, it refers to someone who enjoys food, knows about it and eats and drinks with a certain style and sophistication. It is a complimentary word, e.g.

. Jackie drives an expensive car. She is a **gourmet** whose car is often seen outside expensive restaurants.

. **gourmet** – as an adjective, it means high class, high quality and expensive, e.g.

. In the Mayfair area of London, there are many **gourmet restaurants**, where you can select **gourmet foods**.

. gray/grey

The spelling '**gray**' and '**grey**' are both acceptable. Most people prefer to write '**grey**'. The word grey refers to 'colour', e.g.

. Jane has beautiful grey green eyes.

In fact, it can be a surname, which is spelled as **Gray**.

. gipsy/gypsy

Both 'spellings 'gipsy' and 'gypsy' are acceptable for this common noun. The word '**Gypsy**' for the proper noun begins with the capital letter 'G'. The proper noun is used, when referring to people known as Gypsies(plural) or their language, e.g.

. **Gypsies** are scattered around the world who maintain a nomadic way of life. Their language is known as **Gypsy** language.

. Some people in the UK prefer a **gipsy** way of life, but wish to be known as travellers.

In the last example gipsy is ⟹ a common noun.

. half

There is some confusion surrounding the use of **half**. It can be used as a noun, a pronoun, an adverb or a determiner. The plural form of the noun half is **halves**.

. when it is used as a noun, meaning two equal sections or parts of something that together comprise it, e.g.

. Flamborough is about two and **a half kilometres** from here.

. One and **a half hours is/are** a long enough time.

'hours' (plural noun) but you can use a singular or plural verb form when the plural noun comes after '**half**'. Some people prefer to use the singular form of the verb in such cases: . Sara had a **half** loaf.

> . when it is used as a determiner, it means 'being a half' or 'almost a half', e.g.
>> . From here the rail station is **half** a mile along this road.

'**a**' or '**the**' **is** not needed before **half** when half is functioning as a determiner.
> . We were at the airport for **half** an hour before they arrived.

half is functioning as a determiner↵ - no need for **a** or **the** before **half**

> . when it is used as a pronoun, it means an amount equal to half, e.g.
>> . Due to heavy snow, **half of the class** is absent.

> when used as a pronoun '**of**' is required↵
> . Adam claimed for **half of the property** which two brothers inherited.

. **when it is used as an adverb, it indicates to the extent of half,** e.g.
> . Tonight the hall is **half** full.
> . The loan is only **half** paid as at today.
> . The plastering job is only **half** finished.

These three examples demonstrate that there is no need for placing either '**a**' or '**the**' before **half** when it is used as an adverb.

. **hardly**

See ⇒barely

. **hopefully**

It is an adverb that is used in two different ways as exemplified below:
> . It can mean 'in a hopeful manner something will happen', or 'with hope'. When it is used to express this meaning, it is considered correct use, e.g.
>> . I will be at the conference tomorrow. 'Will you be there?' I asked Colin hopefully.
>> . We were waiting for our exams results **hopefully** on that day.

. The other rather recent use of hopefully is to say 'it is hoped', e.g.
> . **Hopefully**, I will be there.
> . **Hopefully**, we will meet them tomorrow in Red Square, Moscow.

When it is used in this way, many people dislike it, because they consider this use of hopefully incorrect. In fact, most people use **hopefully** in this way. It is now acceptable, at least, in informal contexts.

. **however**

It is an adverb. It can mean nevertheless, on the other hand, but, yet, regardless or to whatever degree. You can place it in the front or in the mid position in a construction. Its usage is demonstrated below:
.   There were thousands of demonstrators against the invasion of Iraq.
    However, the police arrested only three people.

introducing a statement that contrasts with the statement made in the first sentence

. In the following example, **however** is beginning a second clause within the same sentence. <u>In such constructions, it must be preceded by a semicolon and followed by a comma.</u>
    .   There were widespread rumours about his ill-health**; however,** he
        showed no sings of failing health during the performance tonight.

. **I**
See ⇒ between(... me/I)

. **illusion**

It means something is false or non-existent, e.g.
    .   She told me that before she left her husband she had
            <u>no illusions about her feelings for him.</u>

    she did not love her husband ↵
    .   The existence of a true form of democracy in any part of the world
            is an **illusion**.

it implies that a true democracy does not exist anywhere in the world

See ⇒ allusion

. **impracticable/impractical**

Both impracticable and impractical are adjectives and cause some confusion to many writers. <u>**Impracticable** refers to something that is impossible, not workable. It can be achieved or done but it would require a great deal of</u>

effort and more resources than it is worth, e.g.
  . Your innovatory idea is great but it is financially **impracticable**.

Note - It is an appropriate word when you want to emphasize a reason or
reasons for not doing something because you cannot justify it on the basis of
its worthiness.
  . <u>impractical</u> - it can render two different following meanings:
      . <u>**when you want to express that something is unrealistic , not
        serious or cannot be done at all,**</u> e.g.
      . It is **impractical** to complete this project within ten weeks.
      . The criminal thought he would get away, but it was **impractical**.
  . <u>**when you want to say that someone is not good at doing things
    physically**</u>, e.g.
      . My husband is a very good teacher. However, he is hopelessly
        impractical, that is why we have to employ a tradesman to fix this
        door.

. <u>**impractical**</u>
See ⇒ impracticable/impractical

. <u>**in spite of**</u>

As stated under **'despite'**, this phrase has the same meaning as despite.
Like despite, it is also used with a noun or a gerund, e.g.
  . **In spite of** the harsh realities of life, I am still here and contented.
  . **In spite of having** no time to spare, she came to say goodbye to me.
  . **In spite of I** <u>was ill on that day,</u> I attended the emergency meeting.

it is wrong to use in spite of in front of **a finite clause** ⇒ I was ill ---

. <u>**isn't**</u>
        Short form of ⇒ is not

. <u>**its/it's**</u>
    . **its** – determiner <u>and</u> . **it's** is a short form of ⇒ it is <u>and</u> it has

. <u>**inward /inwards**</u>

            . **inward** - it is an adjective . **inwards** - it is an adverb

. **inward** can mean inner feelings or directed towards the middle/
centre of something' or into something, e.g.
  . She is a very calm lady. It is not easy to guess her inward thoughts.
  . Our **inward goods** stores are next to our main factory in Luton.
            ⇑
goods directed/sent to the centre where goods are received

. **inward**s – it means towards the centre or middle of something, e.g.
            . Usually, windows open **inwards**.
      towards the inside of the building↵

. **inwards** can also be used to mean inside yourself, e.g.
  . Since she received a letter from her son, her thoughts turned **inwards**.

. inward-looking

It refers to a person who is not in the least interested in other people, e.g.
  . We can invite David. In fact, he is rather **inward-looking** and does
    not get on well with others.

. inwards
See ⇒ inward /inwards

. jargon

Every subject has its own terminology, technical terms or specialized language. Of course, this specialized language is most suited for communication between subject experts or those who are interested in a particular subject. It becomes a **jargon** when a particular subject specialist is using it to communicate with non-subject experts or the general public. For instance:
  . *Within one LAN or within a local collection of LANs and*
    networked mainframes, which is often called a 'domain',
    it is not necessary to use the full IP host name.
It will be considered as **jargon** in general language. On the other hand, it makes sense to computer scientists and students.

. judicial/judicious

Both are adjectives but have contrasting meanings as illustrated below:
The word **judicial** is used in connection with a court of law, e.g.
        . My Member of Parliament will ask the Prime Minister for a
        judicial review.

. The word judicious means someone showing good judgement, sense or
  prudence, e.g.
       . Our managing director promoted me to the post of manager because
       my timely decisions at work proved to be **judicious**.

. kind of

The word **kind** can function as an adjective as well as a noun. It is a common
word, but it can be a source of confusion to many writers. The way it is often
used in speech is not always grammatically correct. The following examples
illustrate its correct usage:
     . when functioning as a noun – it means a particular variety or type of
     something. It is incorrectly used, when the writer is not thinking whether
     it should be treated as a **countable** or **uncountable noun**, e.g.
          . What **kind of** book do you market?

uncountable noun⏎ kind $\Rightarrow$ singular noun

. When 'kinds of'' is preceded by a plural determiner(these, those ..),
  it is followed by a plural countable noun. This is exemplified below:
     . These **kinds** of apples grow in England.
countable noun⏎ - kinds $\Rightarrow$ plural noun

     . My children used to watch **those kinds** of television programmes.
               used as countable noun ⏎ - plural form of kind $\Rightarrow$kinds
In this case, **those kind** $\Rightarrow$ **grammatically incorrect**

. When kind (kinder, kindest) is functioning as an adjective, it means
  generous, affectionate, friendly, caring about someone or benevolent, e.g.
     . They have been very **kind to** me recently.
     . Please convey my **kindest** regards to your parents.
See $\Rightarrow$sort

. kindly

It can function as an adverb or adjective. As an **adverb**, it means in a friendly
way, or in a humane way, e.g.
     . They have **kindly** accepted our offer of loan payment
        by twelve monthly instalments.
     . He is so annoyed that he would not **kindly** listen to our complaint.

. As an **adjective,** it means helpful, good-natured, benevolent or sympathetic.

You can use it as an adjective only before a noun, e.g.
. A **kindly** passenger helped me by carrying my heavy suitcase downstairs.

. **latter/former**

These words require a careful construction of clauses or sentences in order to avoid confusing the reader and sending the reader back to read again, what he/she has already read. It is best not to overuse these words. **Former** and **latter** do not mean the same, just the opposite as outlined below:

. **former** – It is an adjective but it can be used as a pronoun. When it is used as an **adjective**, it can express a variety of meanings:
. it can refer to something that existed in an earlier time or period, in the past time or old time, e.g.
. Queen Victoria was the empress of the **former** British Empire.
. As an adjective, it can point to something that had some sort of status, fame, glory in the past time, e.g.
. After the reunification of Germany in 1990, many historical buildings in the **former** East Germany were restored to their **former glory**.
. As an adjective, it refers to the first of two people or things previously mentioned, e.g.
. I informed the customer, 'if you order online, you can claim 25% discount or buy through the post. Which of these methods do you prefer?' The customer said, 'the **former** method is acceptable.'
being the first of two methods↵
. when it is used as **a pronoun**, it refers to the first of two people or things previously mentioned, e.g.
. We were informed by the booking clerk that we could choose between a double room on the third floor or an en-suite on first floor. Which one will you take? We will take **the former**.

. **latter** – it can be either an adjective or noun.
. as an **adjective** it refers to something that is the second of two things or people previously mentioned, e.g.
. I will be visiting France and Germany. Which of these countries will be your first stop? The **latter** country will be my first choice as I have already made some arrangements with my clients.

. as a **noun 'the latter'** refers to something that is the second of two things or people previously mentioned, e.g.
> . The maps shows two routes namely A and B. A is longer but it has attractive countryside. Route B is much shorter. I think we should take **the latter**.

Both **former** and **latter** must not be used for a list that contains more than two items. The reason is that both these words refer to <u>one item out of two items only.</u>

See ⇒sort

. leading question

This phrase is often used wrongly to describe a question as hostile, intimidating, difficult to answer, awkward or embarrassing. In fact, it means a question raised in such a way that the questioner prompts you to give the answer that is desired by the questioner, e.g.
> .Yesterday afternoon, you left the office at about 16.00 hours, didn't you?
> **Instead of asking a neutral question**
> . Did you leave the office at about 16.00 hours yesterday afternoon?

. legible/readable

These words are often used incorrectly. The common mistake is to use readable for legible. In fact, these words are not interchangeable.

. **legible** – it is an adjective. It is used in connection with only printed or written words. when a piece of writing can be deciphered, or it is possible to read it, then it is legible, e.g.
> . She writes so small that her writing is scarcely **legible**.
> . Your cheque was in my pocket when it rained and it got wet, however, the writing is still **legible**.

. **readable** – it is also an adjective. It is used to mean that the writing is interesting, enjoyable. It indicates a favourable opinion about a piece of writing, or book, e.g.
> . I do not find this book **readable** because it is too technical for me.
> . I find Smith's regular column in this newspaper **readable** but my wife dislikes his style.

. lethal

See ⇒fatal under fatal/fateful as fatal also pertains to death

. licence/license

These words often cause some confusion. The word **licence** is a **noun**. It is a document issued by the authority to show that a business or someone is authorised to do something in accordance with the law, e.g.
. I have just received my first full driving **licence**.
. You must apply for a licence to sell wines, spirits and cigarettes.

On the other hand, the word **license** is a **verb**. It means to give a business or someone permission to do something in accordance with the law, e.g.
. This shop is **licensed** to sell wines, spirits and cigarettes.
. Market traders are **licensed** by the area local council.

.license

See ⇒licence/license

. majority/minority

These words have opposite meanings but both are singular nouns. The word **majority** means more than half of a group of people or things that can be counted, e.g.
. The **majority** of residents in this area will vote for me.
. The **majority** of personal computers in the world are operated by some operating systems supplied by Microsoft – the world's largest software company.
. **minority** – it means less than half of the total number of people or things in a group, e.g.
. We won because only **a minority** of the Transport Committee voted against our proposal.
. There were about one hundred thousand demonstrators. Only a tiny **minority** caused a disturbance and the police arrested a few.

I would rather avoid using these words and express myself in a different way. For instance:
. **A large majority of our club members** wine and dine in our restaurant.

It can be re-written in a better style and to avoid any ambiguity as:
. **Most our club members** wine and dine in our restaurant.

. It is important to remember that both words **cannot** refer to only a single thing. It must be a group, irrespective of how large or small the group is.

For instance:

. **The majority of the newspaper** does not interest me.

this is wrong because a newspaper is only one thing

. **Majority** and **minority** refer to a group of people or things, e.g. family, crowd, herd of cows, etc. These are collective nouns. After these nouns, the verb can be either singular or plural. Since they represent a number of people or things, it is preferable to use a plural verb after any of these words.
    . The majority of students **were/was** keen to travel to Paris.
    . Only a small minority of conference delegates **were/was** absent after the lunch.

See ⟹ collective nouns in the grammar part of the book

. **male**
See ⟹gender/sex

. **may**

The use of the modal verb may indicates rather a formal circumstance. It is a more polite way to ask for permission, giving or refusing permission. Here are some examples:
    . **May** I be permitted to ask you a question? (polite and formal)
    . Students **may not** park their vehicles in the staff car park.

    official notice ↵
In modern English **mayn't** is wrong. The correct form is **may not**. May is used in official notices in connection with authority and permission.

. **The modal verb 'may' can also be used to express some other meanings,** e.g.
    . She **may have lost** her way to this office. (a doubtful situation)
    . **She may be wealthy** but she has been seen shopping at charity shops.

first accepting that something is true then giving another point of view about the same person or thing
See ⟹ can(and may)

. **me**

See ⟹ between (...me/I)

. **media (the)**

Media is a plural form of the noun **medium**. It can be followed by either a singular or a plural verb. It is a very much overused word that covers radio, television and the newspapers for information and entertainment purposes. It is best to avoid using it and be more specific, e.g.

    . The armed robbery in our small town was reported in the **media**.
    . The media **was/were** warned by the trial judge, when some reporters
      disclosed a vital piece of information which could influence the final
      outcome of this trial.

It would be better to specify which part of the media – newspaper(s), a radio station, etc.

. **minority**

See ⟹ majority/minority

. **misuse**

It has a similar meaning as abuse but the context in which it is used is dissimilar. It expresses a wrongdoing which has an element of dishonesty. It can also mean wrongly applying someone's skills, or using something without permission. For instance:

    . In the UK, senior civil servants hardly ever **misuse** power for their
      own benefit.
    . In many organisations, the use of the internet by members of staff
      for their own purpose, is regarded as misuse of employers' resources.

See ⟹abuse

. **myself**

It is a reflexive pronoun (see pronouns). Some writers use it unnecessarily instead of '**I**' or '**me**', e.g.

    (1) . Please telephone **myself**.
    (2) . My son and **myself** will be travelling by car.

In both examples, the use of a reflexive pronoun is not required. In example 1, it should be replaced by '**me**' objective pronoun, first person. In example 2, it should be replaced by '**I**' subjective pronoun , first person.

Other reflexive pronouns should not be used instead of subjective and objective pronouns.

See ⇒ reflexive pronouns

. need

See ⇒ Modal verb

. neither

It can function as a determiner, a pronoun or as an adverb. It is often incorrectly used. It expresses negative meanings in negative statements.

. when it is used as a **determiner** or **a pronoun**, it means not one nor the other (of two) things or people, e.g.
> . **Neither** brother is at home.
> . **Neither** question is difficult to answer, if you have revised your class notes.
> . **Neither** report highlighted local social problems.

In these examples, neither is followed by **a singular noun** referring to each of two persons and things because we are making negative statements about both of them.
> . **Neither of us** is rich enough to retire prematurely.
> . **Neither of them** is interested in this sort of play.
> . **Neither of these** jackets suits me.

. **Neither** and 'neither of'' agree with the singular verb. When neither can take either a singular or a plural verb is discussed under **neither --- nor** below.

. when it is used as **an adverb**, it indicates that both parts of the negative statement are true. In this way, it modifies the sentence, e.g.
> . I have not written to Anne since June and **neither had Anne**.

           ⇑   ⇑

part 1 of the statement - **true**   part 2 of the statement – **true**

. **Neither can be used on its own when answering to a question,** e.g.
> . Does she reply 'yes' or 'no'? **Neither**.
>   implying no answer was given↵

See ⇒ nor (for a special use of neither)

. neither --- nor---

Neither --- nor is a pair of correlative conjunctions. See conjunctions in the grammar part of the book. This pair of conjunctions is used in negative statements to refer to two alternatives that are not possible, e.g.
. Unfortunately, I have **neither** my visa card **nor** my cheque book with me.
. He is gravely ill. He can **neither** see **nor** hear.
. **Neither** Key **nor** Colin was at home when I telephoned them.

. When does 'neither' agree with the plural verb form?

If the noun after '**nor**' is plural then '**neither**' agrees with the plural verb form, e.g.
> . Most people think that **neither** politicians **nor** their advisers
>   **are** honest enough to be trusted.
> . **Neither** parents **nor** children have arrived.

See ⇒nor/or

. nevertheless /nonetheless

These words are adverbs and mean the same that is 'in spite of all that has been said'. For instance:

. We did not have very much time to catch our last train. **Nevertheless/ nonetheless**, we ran as fast as we could and managed to catch it.
. It was a fatal motorway car crash involving about forty cars. **Nevertheless/ nonetheless** only two people died.

. nice

It is an adjective. It means amiable, friendly, likeable, agreeable, good, enjoyable or pleasant. Some people do not consider it as suitable for business writing and prefer another descriptive adjective. It does not mean you should always avoid using it in writing. You can make use of it in social letters without any hesitation, e.g.
. It was a **nice surprise** to see you at the conference. (meaning pleasant)
. It would be **nice** if you visited us.   (meaning agreeable)

. none

The word **none** can function as either an adverb or a pronoun. When it is functioning as a pronoun, it means there is not a single person or thing, e.g.

. We were expecting some overseas delegates but **none** attended.
. We invited both the chairperson and secretary but **none** accepted our invitations.

. When it is functioning as an adverb, it is followed by the definite article 'the' and a comparative adjective to mean 'not at all' or 'no degree'. The actual sense is derived from the context and the comparative adjective used, e.g.
    . He told me about his financial difficulties but I am still **none the wiser**.

In this example, 'none the wiser' is implying 'still not satisfied with the information given'.

    . Joan was one of the hostages but she is **none the worse** for her ordeal.

    implying she is not suffering or in a bad condition.↲

. **none of something**

This expression is used to quantify something specific, e.g.
. **None of** these shirts fit me any more.
. **None of** the students has/ have enough money to fly to Moscow.

. Should you use a singular or a plural verb form with the expression, ' none of something'?

In fact, there is some confusion about the verb form agreement with this expression. Some writers (dictionaries included) prefer to use with it a singular verb. This is, certainly, the case in formal contexts. In informal situations, a plural verb is usually used. The reason for using a singular verb is that '**none**' is a singular pronoun, e.g.
                        . None of the students **has** a motor car.

. Some writers suggest that 'none' can be used with either a singular or a plural verb, e.g.
    . None of the students **has/have** very rich parents in my class.

. It is best to use a verb form according to the noun or pronoun that comes after ' **none of** ' in the following ways:
    . when the noun is uncountable, use a singular verb, e.g.
        . None of the **equipment is** insured against theft, etc.
        . None of the village **people** has ever experienced such a vast natural disaster in their living memory.

. when the noun or pronoun is plural use either a singular or a plural verb, e.g.

    . None of **these accidents** would **has/ have** happened if drivers
        were warned earlier.

. nonetheless

See ⇒nevertheless/nonetheless

. nor/or

These words need special attention as they are used with **either**, **neither** and without them in a variety of ways.

. **nor** – when you want to link negative clauses, you can use 'and nor' or 'nor', e.g.

    . We could not afford to stay in a 'Four Star Hotel' **and nor**
        could the other passengers on our coach.
    . Most people in this country are not poor, **nor** are they rich.

. You can start a sentence with **'nor'**, e.g.
. Our firm do not export to the European Union. **Nor** do we trade with Japan.

. In some constructions, depending on the context, **'nor'** can be
  replaced by **'or'**, e.g.

    . Due to Christmas celebrations, banks will not open on Friday, **nor**
        Saturday, **nor/or** Sunday **nor/or** Monday.

This example also illustrates that when **nor/or** should be placed before every one of the words to which either **'nor'** or **'or'** refers.

. You can use **'or'** when you wish to state two alternatives, e.g.

    . We can travel by Euro Coach Service **or** by Euro Tunnel.

. A clause beginning with a participle can be linked to the previous
  clause by **'or'**, e.g.

    . She will not be alone travelling with a group of students **or**
        accompanying us. (accompanying = participle)

See ⇒either ---or--- **Also** See ⇒neither --- nor---

. one another

See ⇒ each other/one another

. **onward/onwards**

These words are not interchangeable. The word 'onward' is an adjective but 'onwards' is an adverb. These words are used in different contexts as outlined below:
. **Onward** – it means moving forward, e.g.
      . This tariff includes your return rail return journey to London and onward rail travel to Dover.
. **Onwards** – it indicates the continuation of time from a particular time, or moving on towards a particular direction , e.g.
      . The polling station will open from 7.00 hours **onwards**.

These are rather incomprehensible words. It is best to avoid using them.

. **onwards**

See ⟹ onward/onwards

. **or**

See ⟹ either--- or--- See ⟹ nor/or

. **oral/verbal**

Both words mean the use of words. **Oral** is spoken as opposed to written. **Verbal** is also spoken, not written. In order to avoid any misunderstanding over the meaning of these words, it is best not to describe agreements using these words. It is more common in these days to say 'spoken agreement' and 'written agreement', e.g.
      . Both parties have already confirmed their spoken agreement by exchanging copies of their written agreements.

Verbal is also used in relation to skills and instructions, e.g.
      . The job applicant must pass a verbal test in order to demonstrate his/her good verbal skills.
      . She has to pass both oral and written tests in French.

. **over/under**

In connection with money, it is suggested to avoid using these words and instead state money or numbers as 'more than 'or 'less than', e.g.
     . The total cost will be less than £20.00. This delivery charge will be less than £5.00.

. particular

This is rather a misused and an overused word. It can function either as a noun or an adjective. When it is used as an **adjective**, it means one individual person, thing or type of something which differs from some other types. It should be used only when it is adding some specific further information, e.g.
> . You must pay <u>particular attention to our safety regulations</u>.
> . Any particular car, sir?

In the last sentence, the use of particular is unnecessary because it is not adding any specific information. Its plural **noun** form 'particulars' is used, meaning written information about job, business, etc. For instance:
> . We would require particulars of your employment during the last three years.

. perquisite/prerequisite

These are two very different words but often are a source of some confusion. **Perquisite** is a noun. It is generally labelled as **'perks'**. It means some special payment in forms other than money, such as a company car, free telephone at home, free holiday, etc. For instance:
> . I have a company car that I can use seven days a week for my own private purposes, that is a considerable perquisite.

Prerequisite is a **noun**. It means an essential requirement/condition before something can be done or happen, e.g.
> . A teaching qualification is an essential prerequisite for a teaching post.

Prerequisite is also an **adjective**, but only when it is used before a noun, e.g.
> . We do not require any **prerequisite** skills as we train all our employees.

. practice/practise

Practice is a noun and practise is a verb. For this reason, they are not interchangeable.
> . You must have some **practice** before the final match. ⇐ noun
> . Jane practises her singing skills everyday. ⇐ verb

. practise
See ⇒ practice/practise

. prerequisite
See ⇒ perquisite/prerequisite

. principal/principle

Both words are nouns but have different meanings. **Principal** – it means the head of some institution, or business, e.g.
  . Our college **principal** will retire next Friday after 40 years service.

Principle – It can be used in a variety of ways. It can mean a rule or moral
               in which you believe. It can be used to refer to a scientific law
               or a reason for doing something, e.g.
                             . It is against my **principle** to drink alcohol.

. principle
See ⇒ principal/principle

. purposely/purposefully

Purposefully and purposely are adverbs but they are not interchangeable because they have very different meanings. Purposefully is derived from pur-
poseful(adjective), meaning '**determination**'. Its adverb is purposefully,
meaning '**determinedly**', e.g.
  . My discussion with him revealed that he was acting **purposefully**.

On the other hand, **purposely** is derived from purpose(noun), meaning '**on
purpose**' or '**deliberately**', e.g.
  . Having listen to your side of the story, it appears that he **purposely**
    blocked your entrance to the house.

. purposefully
See ⇒ purposefully/purposely

. questionable

Something is questionable when you have some doubts or suspicions about it
because it may be untrue, dishonest or incorrect, e.g.
      . His reasons for not regularly attending Psychology lectures is highly
       questionable.
      . The information is **questionable** on the ground of inconsistency.
See ⇒ debatable(and questionable)

. quite

It is an **adverb** and deserves an explanation because some people over use it.
It has two meanings:

1) . It can mean fairly, rather, pretty, e.g.
- . She felt **quite tired** and went to bed early tonight.

2) . It can mean completely, absolutely, considerably, entirely, etc.
- . She was **quite prepared** to pay by cash for this purchase.
- . He is **quite** a generous businessman.

In the last example, '**quite**' is used as an **intensifier** (highest degree) before an adjective (active) that precedes the noun (person). When it is used with an adjective before a noun, it comes before the indefinite article (a or an).

. readable

See ⟹ legible/readable

. reflexive pronouns

See ⟹ myself above and reflexive pronouns under pronouns

. relatively

See ⟹ comparatively

. responsible

It means someone whose duty/task is to get something done or care for someone or something, and gets the blame for everything that goes wrong. **Accountable** and **responsible** mean much the same, but they are used to express different life situations. Often **responsible** is used to state less serious situations which do not involve crime and law, e.g.

- . Children under a certain age cannot be held **responsible for** their wrong actions.

See ⟹accountable

. ridiculous

It is an adjective, meaning something silly, or unreasonable. It is not as strong as absurd (see absurd), e.g.
- . Some guests arrived wearing **ridiculous** costumes.

. scarcely

See ⟹barely

. sex

See ⟹gender/sex

. **should**

See ⇒would

. **some**

See ⇒any

. **so**

It can be used as a conjunction. As an adverb, it is overused as an intensifier,
e.g.   . We are **so** pleased to see you again. ⇐ intensifier **so**
As a conjunction, it is less used than '**therefore**' that has the same meaning.

. **sort**

See ⇒kind of

. **stationary/stationery**

Often spellings of these words lead to misuse. **Stationary** is an adjective,
meaning not moving, fixed, motionless, e.g.
    . My car was stationary when the accident happened.

On the other hand, the word **stationery** is a noun. It means writing materials
for both home and office use, e.g.
    . Is there a stationery shop in this area?

. **subsequent**

It is an adjective. It is likely to be confused with the word 'consequent'.
It means happening after something has happened, e.g.
    . Our guests arrived without any prior arrangements and their
      subsequent quick departure upset our plans.
    . The **subsequent** events proved his famous prediction correct.
See also ⇒ consequent/consequential

. **subsequently**

It is an adverb, meaning something happens later or afterwards, e.g.
    . **Subsequently**, I received a written apology from the chairman.

. **than**

It can function as a preposition or as a conjunction. It has two uses. Its main

use is to link two parts of a comparison or contrast in a sentence, e.g.
. He is taller **than** I am.
. She loves him more than **he** does.

It should be remembered that in order to be grammatically correct, than should be followed by the subject of the second part of the sentence. In both above examples, the subject is shown in **bold style**.

. Its other use is to indicate that something happens soon after
   another occurrence, e.g.
      . Hardly had we started our meeting **than** the chairman fainted.

. that/which

Words **that** and **which** can cause problems. In fact, often Microsoft Word software for word processing suggests the use of either of these, if it finds it inappropriate. It does not mean that the software is always right. Frequently, these words are interchangeable.
. If you ask a question offering a limited choice/alternative, the use of
   'which' is used, e.g.
         . **Which** of the four restaurants is your favourite place?
. If you want to refer to a particular thing, person or whatever, use **which**,
   e.g.
         . Paris or London, **which** has more interesting buildings?

. In some constructions, the use of **that** is required, e.g.
      . Is there any thing **that you** have not told us regarding your
         current job?
      . Is there anything **that** you have not yet declared?

. Use **that** when referring to any person or thing in general, e.g.
      . **What** car did she see in her dreams?

. though (and even though)

Though means the same as **although** which is discussed above. **Though** is usually used informally in spoken English. It is less formal. For instance:
   . **Though** she is shy to express herself, she knows her job very well.

You can use though(and although) at the beginning of a sentence as shown by this example. Note where the comma is placed.

. The printed instructions look simple, **though** it is difficult to assemble it.

it is expressing an opinion ⤶ - it is equivalent to **but**

The last example illustrates that you can use **though,** when you wish to express a contrast between two clauses of a sentence in such a way that the meaning of the previous clause appears less important. Note where the comma is used to separate these clauses in a sentence.

. till
See ⟹ until

. together with

This phrase should be followed by a singular verb, if it refers to 'one person together with another person', e.g.
. Jane, one of my colleagues, <u>together with</u> her mother, is meeting me soon.

. under
See ⟹over/under

. uninterested
See ⟹disinterested/uninterested

. until

Till and **until** are interchangeable in most contexts. The only difference between these words is that **until** is rather formal. Both mean the same, that is up to a point in time when something or an event happens, e.g.
. We waited for your reply **until** I telephoned you yesterday.
. **Until** you pay the full price, the car is not your property.
. I worked alone in the office **till** 19 hours last night.

. verbal

It means expressed in words.
See ⟹ oral

.wake

It can function as a verb as well as a noun.

. Its past tense form ⟹**woke** and past participle form ⟹**woken**

. **When it is used as a verb,** it can mean rouse from sleep, arise, awake or get up, e.g.

> . What time do you usually **wake (up)** over the weekend?
>> stop sleeping↵
> . Our baby was **woken (up)** by the loud music played by
>> our neighbours.
> . During our holiday in India, we **woke(up)** to a clear
>> blue sky everyday.

. In spoken English **wake** is followed by ⟹ **up**

> . **When it is used as a noun,** it can mean aftermath, waves or track left
> on the surface of the water by a vessel, or some other object moving
> through the water, wash or trail, e.g.
>> . There are so many wrecked buildings in our town in **the wake
>> of** an unexpected ferocious storm last night.
>> . This big wave is **a wake**, which is left by our ship.
>>> a trail↵

. **which**

See ⟹ that/which

. **would (and should)**

In modern English, **should** and **would** are used interchangeably, e.g.
> . We **would (or should)** like to accept your kind invitation.
> . I **would** like to assure you that we accept the return of
>> faulty goods within fifteen days from the date of purchase.

Some people do not like such conditional statements and prefer to get to the point without such flattering phrases.

However, if you mean to say 'ought to', use **should**, e.g.

> . It is almost 23 hours. I **should** go home now.
> . We should start our journey from home four hours before
>> the flight in order to avoid any train delays to the airport.

Part 4

Get Down to Communicate

Now is the right place in this book to get down to some written communication.

. <u>Style of addressing the reader</u>

In this day and age, formality in addressing people is somewhat relaxed, but it is still desirable that we are courteous and address people correctly. When you write to a large organisation, it is not always possible to know the name of the recipient. If you try to find the name of the person by telephone, you spend time and money on telephone charges. They can still tell you to write to their company, or a particular department. It is, therefore, common practice to address **business letters** as follows:

Salutation remark (opening remark):   'Dear Sir/Madam,'

and conclude the letter with the **<u>Complimentary remark</u>** (closing remark) 'Yours faithfully,'.

Usually, letters from business to business have names of individuals. In this case, it is customary to address them as follows:

Salutation remark: 'Dear Mr Broomfield,' and conclude the letter with the **<u>Complimentary remark:</u>** 'Yours sincerely,'

. <u>The superscription</u>

It means the name and address that is written on the envelope. If you know the recipient's academic awards, titles, honours or any other distinctions, these should be included in the superscription.

If it is a business letter, and you know the name of the recipient, it is polite to mark the letter for the attention of the individual by writing the name. In addition, if you know the post the recipient holds, write it as well. For example:

> For the attention of Mr G B Smith MSc(Computing)(London)
> Managing Director
> Smith Sportswear PLC
> 1 Smith Road
> Edinburgh
> EH1 1BB

The above superscription has **'open punctuation'**. This is increasingly becoming the acceptable style of addressing correspondence.

For important letters do not use **F. A.O.**(for: **For The Attention of**)

. In a workplace, academic and professional awards and other distinctions awarded are important. These should be included in the superscription, if they are known to you.

. Nowadays the superscription has **open punctuation** – it means <u>no</u> punctuation marks are used.

. Some women prefer not to be known as 'Miss' or 'Mrs'. In a business letter, if a woman does not want to state whether she is married or not, she prefers to be addressed as **'Ms'**, e.g., Ms Barbara Castle. Thus, write

> . in the salutation section: 'Dear Ms Castle,' and
> . in the complimentary section: 'Yours sincerely,'.

. If there is no need for preference, address her in accordance with her status, e.g. 'Professor/ Dr/ Mrs/Miss Sara Brooks', or any other status.

. In important business letters that are usually typed/word processed by a secretary, salutation and complimentary marks may be handwritten by the person signing the letter. Often, a greeting such as 'kind regards' is also added and handwritten. This is a good idea as it shows a personal touch and interest. However, it is not necessary to write it by hand. I would prefer to write these lines myself. It is better to be courteous.

. If you write a business letter to husband and wife: In the salutation section write:

> . 'Dear Mr and Mrs John Taylor,' or
> . 'Dear Mr and Mrs J Taylor,' and in the
> . complimentary remark section: 'Yours sincerely,'

<u>One initial of the husband's first name is written after 'Mrs' as shown above. In the complimentary remark section write: 'Yours sincerely,'.</u>

. Often people address a wife as ' Mrs Palma Taylor' that is incorrect. This
  is a common error. It should be her husband's first name, not her own
  first name, followed by her married surname (husband's surname). The
  growing trend is that a married woman mentions her first name followed by
  her husband's surname. It is becoming acceptable.

. For two or more **business women,** write in the:
      . salutation section: 'Dear Ladies,' and
      . complimentary remark section: 'Yours faithfully,'
. For **one woman** whose surname is not known to you, state in the:
      . salutation section: 'Dear Madam,' and
      . complimentary section: 'Yours faithfully,'
. A **professor**, even if he/she is a doctor and professor:
          . 'Dear Professor Brown,"

. <u>Social letters</u>

Social letters are written to relatives, friends and acquaintances. A get well
letter is a social letter. Letters of invitation and sympathy are also examples
of social letters. These letters are informal letters.

The traditional method of sending a letter is through the postal service in the
world. Since the advent of **electronic mail**, young people are especially enthusiastic about e-mail. Most serious social letter writers still use the postal
system for sending letters and consider e-mail as impersonal and unfriendly.
There is no doubt about the speed of electronic mail, convenience and cost,
but I would consider it only if I had to send an urgent message such as in-
forming my friends about my arrival at their local airport.

It may be that your handwriting has deteriorated. In this case, it is better to
type your letter by using your word processor (typewriters are almost museum pieces). Most social letter writers avoid word processing (or typing) a
letter. A word processed/typed letter is considered to be impersonal and unfriendly. If you have word processed/typed a letter, for whatever reason, it is
polite to add an apology or explanation for doing so. It would be appreciated
by the recipient of your letter.

The handwritten letter, which has indented paragraphs, is always much valued. It is worth mentioning that social letter writing, especially to friends, is a
hobby that requires warmth and respect.

In a social letter, it is customary not to list **qualifications** below the grade of doctor after the name in the subscription (on the envelope). These days, it is **not** wrong, if you write the recipient's qualifications, whatever they are, irrespective of their grades, after the name.

. **Parts of a Letter**

The visual presentation of a good written letter means that it must be set out neatly and in a logical manner. This is achieved by dividing the letter into the following sections:

. **Head section** — This is your printed letterhead part of the paper, followed by the date. If it is not a letterhead paper, write your address in the top right-hand corner, followed by the date. In informal letters, such as letters to your mum or dad, the address is left out altogether.

For overseas correspondence - write your name, address and the date. After exchanging a few letters, you may start with the date written in the top right-hand corner. There is no harm if you start with your name and address or the name of your city followed by your country and the date. There are no rigid rules about it. It is a matter of preference. If you are using a printed letterhead for overseas correspondence, write the date beneath your printed information, in the right-hand side of the paper. If you use an aerogramme - start with the date in the right-hand corner, as there is a box for your name and address on the reverse side of the aerogramme.

. **Salutation remark** — this is where you write, 'Dear…,' or other suitable words. This is also known as the opening section. Below you can find salutations for different relationships. It may be that a relative, boyfriend, girlfriend or even your close friend has a "pet name/nickname" If so, use it in an informal letter (Dear followed by "pet" name).

. **Body section** — this is the main part of your letter. It is divided into paragraphs. The number of paragraphs depends on the length of your letter.

. **Complimentary remark** — this is the closing section, where you finish as 'Yours ….'. A list of complimentary remarks is given below. You can use the one you think it is most suitable for your relationship to the recipient of your letter. It also depends how you feel about the person at the time of writing.

. <u>**Signing off**</u> — put your signature under a complimentary remark.

. <u>**Your name**</u> — there is no need to write your full name under your signature when you write to your relatives and close friends. However, if you write to someone with whom you are not on first name terms, write your name under your signature. Once you have exchanged a few letters with your **pen friends**, there is no need to write your name under your signature.

. <u>**Pages**</u> — some people write on only one side of a sheet of paper. It is also perfectly acceptable to write on both sides of the same sheet of paper. When your letter has more than one sheet, it is better to number the pages, so that it is easy to read. Usually, the first page is not numbered. So, start the numbers from 2. Some people write page numbers in the centre of the page but on top of the head section. Some writers prefer to write it in the right-hand top corner, just above the head section.

. <u>Salutation and complimentary remarks</u>

In fact, how to begin and end a letter depends on the following:
> . your relationship with the person
> . how well you know the person
> . how you feel about the person

The following suggestions are based on many years of letter writing experience. It is worth remembering that social letter writing is informal. Therefore, the basic rule for this type of writing is <u>informality,</u> as opposed to formality. Thus, you can use any of the following suitable remarks without any hesitations.

Relationship: Parents, Grandparents, Sisters, Brothers

Salutation Remarks: "Dear Mum,", "Dear Dad,", "Dear Mum and Dad,", "Dearest Dad,", "Dearest Mum,", "Dearest Mum and Dad,", "Dear Brother,", "Dear John,", "Dearest Brother,", "Dearest Sister,", "Dearest Anne,"

Complimentary Remarks: "Love,", "With all my love,", "With much love,", "With very best wishes and love,", "With all the best,", "Lots of love,"

Relationship : Aunts and Uncles

Salutation Remarks: "Dear Auntie Jane,", Dearest Sally,",
"Dear Uncle John,", " Dearest John,"

Complimentary Remarks: "Love,", "With all my love,", "With much
love,", "With very best wishes and love,",
"With best wishes,"

Relationship : Wife, Husband, Fiancé, Fiancée, Girlfriend, Boyfriend

---

Salutation Remarks: "Dear David,", "My Darling Susan,", "My Darling
John,", "Dearest Angelica,"

Complimentary Remarks: "Love,", "With all my love,", "With much love,",
"With very best wishes and love,", "With best
wishes,"

Relationship: Sons, Daughters, Nieces, and Nephews

Salutation Remarks: "Dearest Alexander,", "Dear Aristotle,",
"Dear Rachel,", "Dearest Sophia,"

Complimentary Remarks: "Love,", "With all my love,", "With much
love,", "With very best wishes and love,",
"With best wishes,"

Relationship: Youngsters to adults

Salutation Remarks: "Dear Mr Clarke,", "Dear Mrs Clarke,", Dear Mr &
Mrs Brown,"
<u>**When allowed to call by first name**</u>:
"Dear Barry,", "Dear Barbara,"
<u>**Addressing very close old family friends**</u>:
"Dear Auntie,", "Dear Uncle,"

Complimentary Remarks: **"Love,", "With all my love,", "With much**
love,", "With very best wishes and love,",
"With best wishes,"

Relationship: Very close unrelated old friends of your family -
if you call them as "Auntie", "Uncle"

Salutation Remarks: "Dear Auntie Sandra,", Dearest Clair,", "Dear Uncle
Jim,", " Dearest Jim,"

Complimentary Remarks: "Love,", "With all my love,", "With much
love,", "With very best wishes and love,",
"With best wishes,"

Relationship: Close friends

Salutation Remarks: "Dearest Anne,", "My Dear Sigrid,",
"My Dear Beata,", "Dearest Beata,"
"Dearest Jolanta,", "Dear Ines," ,
"My Dear Yvonne,"

Complimentary Remarks: "Love,", "With all my love,", "With much
love,", "With very best wishes
and love,", "With best wishes,", "Lots of love,"
"Kind regards and lots of love,"

Relationship: Acquaintance, or anyone with whom you are not
on first name terms

Salutation Remarks: "Dear Mr Taylor,", "Dear Mrs Taylor,"

Complimentary Remarks: "Yours sincerely,"

Relationship: Pen friends

Salutation Remarks: "Dear Wolfgang,", "Dear Ines,", "Dear Anne,"

Complimentary Remarks: "Yours,",
<u>After an exchange of a few letters, you don't
have to say</u> "Yours,",
<u>Just write:</u>
"Best wishes,", "Kind regards,", "Best wishes
and kind regards,"

. Think about the recipient

The above information lays the foundations for written communication. When you write a letter, think about the person to whom you are about to write. if it is a social letter, the recipient of your letter must be pleased to receive it, and enjoy reading it. It is not always possible to give some good and exciting news, but the way you describe things can be interesting. Therefore, try not to impress the recipient with too many words which need explanation, but be polite and honest.

There is no need to be afraid of writing a long letter, because some people enjoying reading such letters. Usually, older people like to read and write long letters. They have time for this activity. Young people also enjoy reading such letters. Older children especially like some sort of drawing, such as a smiling face. The content of your letter will reveal how much pleasure you have had in writing it. Here are some examples of social letters:

Congratulations on passing exams from an uncle

> 12 Broad Street
> Manchester
> M1 12 BB
>
> (date here)

Dearest Simon,

I'm delighted to hear the good news that you have passed your final exams for your Bachelor of Science degree. I congratulate you whole-heartedly on your well-deserved success.

It is wonderful that you have gained an upper second class pass, which was required by the company who have conditionally offered you the post of Systems Analyst. Your achievement in the exams has met the employment condition, and it has opened the door for future prosperity. Indeed, you have gained your objectives. It is great news, as you can start your career right away with a reputable large software company. Well done!

I will return home from Switzerland next month, a few days before your double celebration party. Most certainly, it'll be a great pleasure to join you on this happy occasion.

I'm very much looking forward to seeing you all and joining the celebrations.

Love and very best wishes,

Ian

This is to wish a colleague good luck in a new post

3 King Street
Leeds
LE 1 8XX

(date here)

Dear Alistair,

I have just found out from Jane that you have accepted the post of Systems Programming Manager at People's PLC in the City, and you will be soon leaving us. I am ever so pleased that at last you are successful in getting a job which you wanted for a long time. Certainly, it is a promotion at this time in your career. Congratulations!

This is, indeed, a step in the right direction. I hope this chance of working for an international financial institution will give you every opportunity to progress towards becoming Director of Information Systems. This is your final goal, and now you are one more step nearer to it. We all know how hard you work and how much energy you put into it. Obviously, you have done very well.

We will miss you at XYZ, but your new work place is close to us. Once you're settled down in your new post, we could meet, whenever possible, for lunch or a drink, after work, in the same old place as usual.

Let me know how you are coping with your new responsibility, and how you are getting on in general. Do keep in touch!

With very best wishes,

James Baker

The letter writer has a good friendship with the recipient. Their friendship and the informality between them are indicated by both the opening and closing remarks.

Congratulations on the engagement of a close friend

> 12 Palace Road
> Bridlington
> YO 16 3BN
>
> (date here)

My Dear Sarah,

Thank you so much for inviting me to your engagement party on 12 August 2005. It is great news that you have become engaged to John Russell. I have known John for many years, because we both went to the same school. He really is a charming, honest and loving person.

I have seen you and John happy together for nearly two years, and can say that you were made for each other. We can talk about it, when we meet soon, but I must add that I honestly believe you have made the right decision.

I'm very much looking forward to joining your celebration party.

With very best wishes and love,

Karen Smith

The above letter is from a close friend. In such letters, you can say more than just accepting an invitation to an engagement.

. Letters of sympathy

In all our lives, there are occasions when we have to write letters of condolence, following a bereavement. Some years ago, people used to write lengthy letters about the deceased's life. When writing a letter of condolence, it is suggested that you keep your letter short in such a way that you convey your sincere feelings of sympathy to the deceased's relatives in simple words. Any other matters should <u>not</u> be included. You may add a few words about the deceased person, if you feel that you ought to do so. It should be a handwritten letter.

Letter of condolence – death of an acquaintance

> 20 Grove Close
> Nottingham
> NT4 5LD
>
> (date here)

Dear Mrs. Blanket,

I was deeply saddened to read in today's local paper that your beloved husband Lesley was involved in a fatal car accident. Lesley's sudden death has shocked my husband and I. How horrendous for you to lose him, so tragically, so young and so suddenly.

My husband and I offer our sincere sympathy on your loss.

With kindest regards,

Yours sincerely,

Janet Baker

The following letter is slightly longer than the previous one. The reason is that the writer knows how much the recipient would like to hear from him, as he knew his friend's wife well.

Letter of condolence – death of a close friend's wife

> 35 Cross Road
> London
> NW1 9 QL
>
> (date here)

My Dear John,

Last night, my mother broke the dreadful news of Jane's death over the telephone. Anne and I are shocked. I can't imagine how sorrowful you are on your beloved wife's death. If it's any consolation, she has been finally released from her painful illness.

Anne and I enjoyed her friendship for so many years. She was always ever so kind, honest, cheerful and helpful. Jane was always very hospitable to friends and strangers. We will miss her very much.

If there is anything at all which we can do to help, please ask us without any hesitation.

We send you our deepest sympathy.

Love,

Anne and Dan

. Hospital visit

When you write to a colleague, an acquaintance, or a friend with whom you do not have a very close relationship, it is not easy to say whether you should visit them or not. The problem is that for some reasons, they may not want visitors other than their relatives and intimate friends. On the other hand, they may appreciate your visit as very few people visit them. Anyway, it is a good idea to indicate that their work has been taken care of and there is no need to worry about it. Furthermore, it is advisable to add that you will be happy to help if they ask you.

Letter of sympathy – a colleague in hospital

12 Blackburn Road
Burnley
BU 5 9 NN

(date here)

Dear Craig,

I'm sorry to hear that you had been admitted to Chelsea & Kensington Hospital for an emergency operation, but luckily, there were no complications. It is such a big relief to learn that the operation was successful and you're making satisfactory progress.

There is no need to worry about work, as the manager has already organised cover for you for as long as you are away due to illness. If there is anything at all which I can do to help, please let me know.

I hope that you will be fully recovered from your operation soon.

With kindest regards,

Andrew Brown

You can write a similar letter to someone who has had an accident and is unable to work.

. Get well messages

If a friend or relative is ill, you can send a get well message. You can buy specially designed get well cards with a variety of printed messages. It is a matter of taste and how you feel about the sick person. These cards have sufficient space to write a short personal note. So, you may send a card with your handwritten note on it. If you do send a card, it is recommended that you choose a card which does not refer to an illness on its front, as it may prove to be depressing. It is better to buy a card with some sort of alternative picture or design. If you don't send a card, you can still send a message written on a sheet of ordinary writing paper. Here is an example:

Get well message from colleagues sympathising about illness

Work Place address Printed

(date here)

Dear Ray,

Here in the IT Department, we are all very sorry to learn that you are unwell and wanted to let you know that we are thinking of you.

Monika and Barbara are providing cover for you until you are back. Therefore, don't worry about work, just look after yourself. We will be pleased to see you back at work, when you are fully recovered from your illness.

With best wishes,

Signed by colleague in Accounts

. Invitations

Nowadays, an increasing number of people send invitation cards, telephone, fax or exchange e-mail messages. All modes of communication except the ordinary telephone still involve some writing. It also depends on the nature of the invitation. If you want to invite a few close friends for a drink in a local pub, you can telephone them. For other occasions, it is a good idea to have something in writing because it is still valued.

Invitation to a house-warming party
(informal letter)

(date here)

Dear Alison and Arthur,

Last month, we moved to our new home. It wasn't quite as simple as we thought it would be. It was rather a hectic experience but we are glad that it's all over now. Our new address is:

> "Sea view Cottage"
> The Square
> Flamborough
> YO18 6JJ

Telephone: 01262 500 5000   Fax: 01262 500 5001

Albert and I invite you to join us to celebrate the move and to toast our new home on Saturday 4 June. A bit of knees-up will kick off at about 21.00 hours. We would be delighted if you could come along! Hope to see you on Saturday.

With best wishes,

Edna and Albert

. Replying to invitations

It is straightforward to accept an **informal invitation**. You should reply as soon as you can, so that the host has a good idea of the number of people who will participate in the event. This is illustrated below:

Acceptance of an invitation to a house-warming party

45 Ramsgate Road
Bridlington
YO 16 7 BN

(date here)

Dear Edna and Albert,

Thank you very much for inviting us to your house-warming party. Indeed, we would be ever so pleased to come. We know the area where your new house is situated very well. It is a really nice district. Well done!

Look forward to seeing you at about 8.30 p.m. on Saturday 4 June.

With our very best wishes,

Alison and Arthur

If you have **to decline an informal invitation** for whatever reason(s), it is important that you do so politely without any unnecessary delays. Your friendly letter will not offend them.

A letter of refusal to join a house-warming party

> 45 Ramsgate Road
> Bridlington
> YO 16 7 BN
>
> (date here)

Dear Edna and Albert,

Thank you very much for inviting us to your house-warming party. I'm very sorry that I will not be able attend it, as I have already bought my train ticket to visit my parents in Blackpool.

As they are anxiously waiting for my long overdue visit, I cannot give it a miss. Your social gatherings are always joyful and I hope that you and your guests have a great time on Saturday 4 June.

When I'm back from Blackpool, I'll ring you up so that we can arrange to meet for a drink.

With our very best wishes,

Colin

. **Far away friends**

You may start as a pen friend, and steadily develop your friendship into a family friendship. It all depends on trust and a genuine desire to understand each other, to exchange points of view and life experiences in general. Indeed, it is a very pleasing hobby. It can brighten your day when you hear from a far away friend. It can enable you to relax, as you learn to share your feelings, etc. with your friends. Indeed, through letters, one learns that we can be united by a sense of common humanity.

A letter to develop a friendship with someone you met on holiday

Address
in
England

(date here)

Dear Sylvia and Ralf,

I just thought of you as I was working on my PC and vividly remembered everything about our short meeting. I decided to stop work, and write this short letter, so that I can convey my feelings to you. How wonderful it was to meet both of you!

The problem is that life on this planet is too short and we are very much involved in maintaining it. The human race is still loveable, no matter where one lives, and what nationality one belongs to. Nationalities are no more than political labels, which unfortunately divide the human race and erect psychological barriers between us. Despite these artificial partitions between people of this global village, it is so enjoyable to accept people from other parts of the world and to share this short life together, whenever an opportunity for meeting arises. We should avail ourselves of life's rare chances of bringing people together, despite geographical distances, different nationalities and gender.

Indeed, our words create a world as we see it. Therefore, we should speak those words, which bring us together as the people who belong to one human race, irrespective of some apparent differences.

I send you this short letter because I feel as if I'm still sitting next to you in that café and talking to you with great enthusiasm with a view to exchanging our experiences in this present life, and indeed, sharing world heritage as well as improving our mutual understanding.

To maintain our lives on this planet, as you may remember, I work for myself as a computer programmer and, therefore, I can work from home. My wife has a part-time job in a department store. I thought you would like to see where we live, thus I have sent you a few snaps. These will give you an idea of our simple but happy life style. We live in the Greater London area, just 10 miles away from Central London. We have the best of both worlds – the capital of the UK and the countryside. We consider ourselves lucky, as we are alive and healthy.

I sincerely hope that it will not be too long before I hear from you.

Kind regards and best wishes,

Yours sincerely,

Tracy White

. **Business letter writing**

Business letterhead paper is official paper which should only be used for official business letter writing, that is, for dealing with business matters. Nowadays, many businesses do not send letters with day-to-day documents such as invoices, accounts statements and the like. Any generalisation of business letter writing in terms of day-to-day routine letters and important correspondence does not apply to all kinds of businesses.

It is of paramount importance that the writer should have precise **factual information** relating to the letter being written. In order to establish all facts, it may be necessary to check all relevant records, telephone conversations or seek information and advice from any other colleague(s) who might have dealt with the matter before.

Depending on the nature of the business and the content of the letter, the writer should use **the language style** that is most suited and it must match the knowledge and understanding of **the recipient**. It is wasteful and confusing to the recipient when you use too many words and jargon/technical phrases or local expressions. It should go without saying that **plain English** is preferred by most people. Of course, if you are a biologist writing to another biologist, your language will include technical phrases, which will not alienate the recipient.

On the other hand, if you use technical words which are commonly used in your trade and write long and verbose sentences, you can easily confuse the recipient who does not possess the knowledge of your trade or profession.

Likewise, if you **oversimplified** your writing, the recipient may feel patronised. Therefore, the best idea is to use plain English, that is to use appropriate words and short sentences that make the point directly, clearly, accurately and briefly. [Note: Plain English is not for toastmasters.] Here are some examples of business letters:

Enquiring about supplies

Letterhead
Business name and address etc.

date here

Sales Manager
XYZ Limited
12 London Road
Birmingham
B1 2BB1

Dear Sirs/Madam,

I understand that your company is the sole distributor for the WWW Publications, which we are interested in stocking.

I would be grateful if you would provide me with a current catalogue of WWW Publications and a retail price list. Please could you also send your trading terms and conditions, together with your discount rates for bookshops and credit account opening information by return of post.

Yours faithfully,

John Smith,
Manager

. The idea is to obtain some relevant information on WWW Publications only. At this stage, you are not interested in some other products.

. Relevant commercial and payment information is requested in the second paragraph, in case, you decide to order some goods. There is no need to give any information on your business, as in the second paragraph the nature of your business is already stated - bookshop.
. If you wish, you can add 'With good wishes' on a separate line above the complimentary remark.

Opening a credit account

Letterhead
Business name and address etc.

date here

Mr R M Henderson
Sales Manager
XYZ Limited
12 London Road
Birmingham
B1 2BB1

Dear Mr. Henderson,

Thank you for your letter of 12 June. We would very much like to stock some of the items listed in WWW Publications current catalogue. We are pleased to send you the following two business contacts whom you can approach for references about our company:

. Mr H N Roberts, Manager, Hope Bank PLC, High Street, Rugby, RB1 2NW

. Miss A Johnson, Credit Controller, ABC PLC, Tree Street, White Cross Reading , RE1 2BC

We await your reply and look forward to doing business with you to our mutual interest.

Yours sincerely,

John Smith,
Manager

. You have decided to open a credit account at XYZ Limited. Since XYZ does not have a formal form for this purpose, you must send two business references. One of these must be your business bank where your current business account is operated from. The following example illustrates how to write this simple letter.

<u>Confirming the opening of a credit account</u>

<u>Letterhead</u>
<u>Business name and address etc.</u>

date here

Mr John Smith
Manager
Vision Bookshop
3 Kensington High Street
London W11 4MN

Dear Mr. Smith,

<u>Reference: Current Account Number: 00123</u>

We are pleased to confirm that your credit account number is **00123** and that your monthly credit limit is **£1,500**.

At present, we do not accept payments by BACS (Bankers Automatic Clearing System). Therefore, all payments should be made by cheque within thirty days from our invoice date.

Yours sincerely,

Miss Doris Day,
Credit Control Manager

. In the above letter, the essential information is given in paragraph 1, so that the trade between these two businesses can commence. In the second paragraph, a polite advance notice is given, so that the supplier is not approached for **BACS** method and to avoid delaying payment. There is no need to add any further information.

. A quotation for goods or services

The acceptance of a quotation forms the basis of an agreement between two parties. Thus, it is advisable to clearly state the nature of your purchase, prices, terms and conditions. Without clear understanding of what is agreed, there can be some problems later. Therefore, it is important to write a precise and concise letter stating all key points.

. In the following example, the **bullet-pointed** list of items gives a job specification (nature of purchase) - things that must be done.
. The next paragraph relates to the date when the work should commence, days to be taken to complete the work and any problems that may arise because of unpredictable weather conditions.
. In the last paragraph, the price is written twice – in both numbers and words. The guarantee is underlined and payment time is stated with the payment condition. Finally, the recipient's attention is drawn to the attached copy of the letter which must be signed and dated by the recipient and returned to the writer.
. If a quotation is about a complex job or some expensive purchase, such as a property deal, it is worth paying a fee to a solicitor, so that the purchase agreement has a proper legal format.

Accepting a quotation

Letterhead
Business name and address etc.

date here

Mr M R Dodd
Director
Dodd Building Services(London) Limited
1 Camden High Street
London NW1 7 AX

Dear Mr Dodd,

Reference: Q123908

Thank you for your quotation for replacing the existing flat roof of our office extension at the above address. We are pleased to accept your quotation for the following work:

. to strip off the existing felt and decking
. to re-board the roof with 18 mm plywood
. to re-felt using 2-layers of built laid bonded hot bitumen, finish
  lay green mineral
. to supply and fix new wooden fascia to all three sides of the roof
. to re-fix all gutters
. to dispose of all waste materials

We understand that the work will commence at about 7.30 hours on 20 July. The job will be completed within three days. If there are any changes due to severe weather conditions before starting the work, you will contact me immediately, so that we can make some other arrangements to complete this job satisfactorily without any unnecessary delays.

The total cost for all materials and work is £3,500 plus 17.5% VAT. This price includes <u>five years guarantee of labour and materials, if within five years any part or the whole flat roof needs any repairs or replacement</u>. The total price three thousand and five hundred pounds plus VAT is payable on the day, when the job is satisfactorily completed as per your quotation and this letter. If you accept the content of this letter, please sign and date the attached and return it to me.

Yours sincerely,

Carl Duncan,
Purchasing Manager

. <u>Rejecting a quotation</u>

The buying department may receive a number of quotations. Often many buyers do not write to prospective suppliers whose quotations are rejected because it is both time consuming and costly. On the other hand, some buyers feel that it is in their business interests to acknowledge all quotations and inform each supplier why their quotation was unacceptable. By using this approach one can also avoid receiving further telephone calls, letters or even salesmen's visits from all those prospective suppliers of goods and services, enquiring and trying to negotiate about the outcome of their quotations. It is suggested that you write a letter to all prospective suppliers who sent you their quotations on the following lines:

. start by acknowledging the receipt of their quotation and state the
quoted price for the proposed goods and service.
. give your reason for finding their quotation unacceptable.
. tell them that at some point in time in the future you will contact them
for some quotations. The tone of this letter should be friendly but its
message has to be regrettably, dismissive.

. <u>Sales letters</u>

Sales letters are not easy to write, yet many people consider them as junk
mail and put them into the waste paper basket without opening them.

The prime purpose of a sales letter is to persuade the recipient to buy some
products or services offered by the writer of the sales letter. For instance, a
small hand written duplicated note from a window cleaner, offering his services, pushed through the letterbox, is a sales letter. When you receive
through the post a large white envelope containing a letter and some glossy
leaflets from a large insurance company, it is also a sales letter. The range of
sales letters is very wide. A sales letter may be disguised as an invitation,
which is well designed and printed in colours on glossy paper. For instance:

> "An invitation to a wine and cheese party and to witness the launch of a
> new and exciting BMW business car at our purpose-built showroom
> in your town ..."

In some sales letters, some ridiculous claims are made. For instance, 'the
most attractive place in the world', 'the cheapest and best', and similar
phrases. You should describe your products or services in words which give
correct factual information and ensure that your products or services can
match their descriptions and stand up to close scrutiny.

<u>A sales letter</u>
<u>Letterhead</u>
<u>Business name and address etc.</u>

<u>date here</u>

Mr G Spencer
Proprietor
Linden Hall Nursery
Linden Hall
YO1 8LH

Dear Mr. Spencer,

I visited your nursery last Sunday afternoon, as we were in your area. It is, indeed, a large nursery, as you have a wide range of all kinds of indoor and outdoor plants, shrubs, bushes and gardening accessories. At your cash desk, four persons were dealing with customers payments and all chargeable amounts were worked out without the aid of any calculating machine. Customers paid by cash and transactions were completed without receipts given to customers. In fact, there was a long queue of customers, including myself, waiting to pay for their purchases.

I do not see anything wrong with this system, but I thought I should write to inform you that we have developed our computer based cash register and management system. This system has been supplied to many retailers and our clients include a number of nurseries in the UK.

Once you have initially invested in this reliable, accurate and fast system, you will soon experience fast cash handling, dealing with credit card transactions, issuing sales receipts, improved and timely ordering of stock items, regular management reports, customer satisfaction and an increase in sales. After some time, the financial benefits will become apparent, as the cost of overall business administration will decrease gradually.

Our system is guaranteed and we service it on a regular basis. I would be happy to introduce you to one of our clients in the nursery business and they will be glad to discuss our system with you.

Our systems consultant and a demonstrator can visit you at your earliest convenience and give you a demonstration without any obligation.

I look forward to hearing from you.

Yours sincerely,

Alan Jolly,
Managing Director

. The communication approach in this letter is based on an observation.
  The first paragraph makes it clear.
. Linden Hall nursery's current system is <u>not</u> criticised.

. Linden Hall nursery's current system is <u>not</u> criticised.
. A link is created between an initial investment in this system and
some key benefits without too much unnecessary emphasis.
. An assurance is given to the prospective customer in terms of the
guarantee, service and a reference.
. The recipient is invited to see a demonstration of this system at the
recipient's own place without any obligation.

On the whole, it is a simple, precise and concise letter. It does not make any
wild claims about the system being offered for sale.

. <u>Money matters</u>

For whatever reasons, sometimes customers do not pay for goods or services
purchased but continue sending orders. In the interest of your business, you
do not wish to upset them but at the same time you must get your payment
from them before they even go bankrupt.

. In the following letter, the writer acknowledges the order from a
customer but politely and firmly rejects it by giving a reason.
. The recipient is reminded of the terms and conditions of trade. Here
the writer firmly informs the recipient that the order will be kept on file
for only ten days. It is also stated that within this period, payment should
be made, so that it can be processed.
. A request from a customer to increase the existing credit limit. Since the
customer's sales account shows that they have not paid for goods
supplied two months ago and have already bought goods equivalent to
the agreed credit limit, it is not your company's policy to increase their
credit limit in such circumstances.

There is no need to tell them something which does not sound right, when a
polite and sympathetic reply is sufficient. However, inform them that you
still value their orders, and you will continue to supply goods within the existing credit limit.

Declining a sales order

Letterhead
Business name and address etc.

___

<u>date here</u>

Mr J M Simpson
Buyer
Bow Electronics Ltd
12 Clapham Common
London
SW12 8 VC

Dear Mr. Simpson,

Thank you for the order number A 00234 received today. Regrettably, your account is already two months overdue. Furthermore, you have already purchased goods equivalent to the agreed monthly credit limit of £5000.

In accordance with our terms and conditions of trade, we would very much appreciate your cheque for £5000 before we can complete this order. We will keep this order on our pending file for ten days. We hope that within this time you will be able to send us a cheque. As soon as we have received your cheque, we will release this order for completion.

Yours sincerely,

Bruce Butler,
Credit Control Manager

. **Employment matters**

It is really important to give serious thought to what you should say in your letter of employment and CV(Curriculum Vitae). A well-written letter of employment and CV can get you an interview but cannot guarantee that you will be successful at the interview. However, your letter of application clears the first hurdle for you, if you get a call for a job interview. Therefore, it is important to prepare both the letter and the CV with great care and thought. A well-written letter does not mean a letter composed as a super literary piece of writing but simple, polite, clear and concise that gives correct information.

. **A CV or *Résumé***

A CV is also known as a ***résumé***. A CV will be read by a number of people. Each person will make an observation. Therefore, you should design a CV that keeps selling your attributes.

. <u>CV styles</u>

There are a number of ways to draw up your CV. In fact, some companies offer a commercial service for preparing your general CV, which you can circulate to prospective employers and employment agencies. This service is not recommended in this book. If your letter of application and your performance at the interview do not match it, you will be very disappointed after the interview.

If you want to compete successfully with other applicants, you must write a CV that meets the requirements of the job for which you wish to apply. It is worth knowing that a style of CV for a young person will not be suitable for someone who has been working for some years and may have changed jobs many times.

It is best to use quality white paper of A4 size. It must be typed/word processed on one side of the page only. Allow left and right margins, as well as at the top and bottom of the page. It is a good idea to avoid excessive use of underlining, or similar emphasis, as some people do not like it.

. In the following example, a CV is drawn for a young graduate applying
  for the post of a graduate trainee. The style is known as **<u>historical.</u>** It
  gives information in a chronological order. It is most suited when
  someone's career or work experience is unbroken. Therefore, this style
  is ideal for young people, as it shows continuity since they left school.
  It is also suitable for people who have not changed jobs over many
  years of their lives.

. The CV must be sent with a covering letter. It is strongly recommended
  that a letter of application is short and precise. It must not be more than
  two pages. Usually, prospective employers set the size - A4 one page,
  one side only.

. Most employers will ask you to fill in an application form. It is important
  that you complete it. A CV and a letter of application are sent together when
  you are directly approaching a prospective employer for a suitable
  employment. If you are granted an interview, it is highly likely that you will
  be asked to fill in an application form.

A CV for a graduate

Personal History

Title: Miss   **Status:** Single

Surname: Scott   **Other Name:** Jane **Date of Birth:** 12.12.1980   **Age:** 21 years

Address: 23 Home Street, London NW1 1BN   **Telephone:** 0123 456 987

National Insurance No. ABC/1334/ABN **Driving Licence:** Full UK **Passport:**
                                                                          Full UK

Health: Excellent **Next of Kin:** Mr and Mrs Scott (parents) at the address shown
                                            above

Objective

A graduate trainee appointment in IT field. I possess BSc(Hons)
Degree in IT and some part-time work experience. I can quickly learn
and contribute towards the IT team work at Goldsmith Retail Stores.

Education

1992- 99	Green Comprehensive School, Camden Town London NW1 2BB
1999 –04	Newland University Bristol BR1 6FD

Qualifications

1997	GCSE in English Language (B), Maths (A), Computer Studies (A), Physics (C), British Constitution (B)
1999	A Levels in Computer Studies (A), English (B), German (C)
2004	BSc (IT), second Class Honours, Newland University

Work Experience

1992–2004	Part-time weekend, Shop Assistant, Foods & Drinks Store Camden Town London NW1 1SD Duties included filling of shelves, stock checking, checkout help and stock taking

cont./

A CV for a graduate (continued from the last page)

2004-to-date Part-time weekend, Shop Assistant,
Friendly Stores
Newton Street, Bristol BE3 5AC
Duties included filling of shelves, stock checking,

Interest & Hobbies

. I played hockey at school and university.
. I held the post of chairman, IT Society at Newland
University

Reference:

Dr Peter Sellers
Head of Computing School
Newland University
Bristol
BR1 6FD

Tel: 0126 44445

Miss J Smith
Store Manager
Foods & Drinks Store
Camden Town
NW1 1SD

Tel: 0207 444 1234

A letter of application for the post of a trainee graduate in IT field

1 Hamilton Road
Bristol
BR 1 9S

(date here)

Miss M B Jones
Personnel Manager
Goldsmith Retail Stores
Paddington
Peterborough
PE1 4AA

Dear Miss Jones,

I have been informed by our Graduate Employment Officer at the University of Newland that annually you recruit some newly qualified graduates. This year, I completed my BSc (Hons) degree in IT. I would very much appreciate it if you would consider me as a candidate.

I am particularly interested in joining your company **because** I have had some part-time experience working in the retail business. During the last twelve years, I worked for two major retail stores in London and Bristol. This experience has given me some working knowledge of big store operations and the important role played by IT in the smooth running of a large retail store.

On my IT degree course, I have experienced theoretical computing and IT knowledge, and acquired some software development skills. I believe that my training at your company will enable me to extend my knowledge and skills as well as to take part in developing software for the company quickly.

 I enclose a copy of my CV and hope that you will grant me an interview.

I look forward to hearing from you.

Yours sincerely,

Jane Scott

Jane Scott

. <u>Faxes (facsimile) and e-mail messages</u>

The greatest advantage of a fax over the post and an e-mail is that it can arrive quicker than even the e-mail message, which can take several hours to reach its destination via the internet networks all over the world. A fax is sent directly from one machine to another machine, which can be a simple fax machine or a computerised fax system. In both cases, the transmitted fax arrives at its destination instantly. Many businesses have designed their own fax/e-mail cover sheet formats so that the recipient can easily identify from where the fax or e-mail has arrived and its subject. If no cover sheet is included, the essential information is given at the top of the sheet on which the message starts.

For business messages to customers, suppliers, etc. one should use the formal language – same as for other business correspondence. Often e-mail messages between colleagues are written in informal style. Messages between friends and relatives can be very informal, depending on the nature of your relationship. There is no need to include salutation and complimentary remarks. You can just sign your name. It may be that your organisation has a particular way of starting and finishing the message, which you must follow. However, it is suggested that you start your message with the basic information under the topics which are in printed in **bold style** in the fax shown below.

. **An e-mail format should include the following essential information**

From: Simon Burk<simonburk@abcinsurance.co.uk>
To: John Major< johnmajor@parliament.org.uk>
Date: 12 May 2005
Subject: Charity Cricket Match

                write your message here

------------------- ------------------------------------- ---------------------
------------------- ------------------------------------- ---------------------
------------------- ------------------------------------- ---------------------

It is best not to write more than 80 characters per line. This way, the chances of text disappearing from the recipient's screen are at a minimum.

. **E-mail communication** has some advantages and disadvantages. These are summarised below:

. **Advantages**

. cheaper means of communication as it costs little and most businesses have an Internet connection for sending and receiving e-mail messages.
. suitable for short messages, such as acknowledging a letter, making appointments and similar tasks.
. global communication is much easier and faster, as it can be delivered any where in the world faster than the postal system.

. **Disadvantages**

. lack of security – you can never be sure who is going to read your confidential information. It can end up where it should not be. Its contents and format can be changed without your knowledge.
. unsuitable for transmitting large files/documents, important documents with symbols, pictures, etc. as they can be distorted due to technical problems.
. on computer screen, documents do not have the same effect as printed

documents. Yes, they can be printed out, but the quality is poorer than the original documents. Often, printed out documents are lifeless, tedious to read and important symbols, etc. may be missing.

. printouts may not be possible if you are travelling with your laptop without the print facility.

A fax

Fax from:	ABC Insurance PLC The Business Centre Queen Street Birmingham BA1 AA	Logo

Telephone: 041 333 1234 Fax: 041 333 1235

Fax to: Mr James Brown, A. D. R. (London) Limited
          Write address(if necessary)
Date: 12 May 2005
Subject: Motor Insurance   **No. of pages**(including this page): 2
From: Jane Smith, Motor Insurance Renewal Dept.
          karensmith@ abcinsurance.co.uk

As per our telephone discussion this morning, page 2 of this fax is a copy of your Motor Insurance Certificate Number 7014444561. This document can be given to the suppliers of your new car, so that they can prove to the Driver and Vehicle Licensing Agency that you are fully insured for driving a motor car. It will enable the suppliers of your new car to register, today, a new motor car with the Driver and Vehicle Licensing Agency in your name.

I am also sending you the original certificate by First Class Registered Post, which you should receive within the next two days.

Karen Smith

The lack of space in this book does not allow me to write beyond this point on this topic.

Glossary

A

a/an - see Troublesome Words and Phrases
a bit - see Troublesome Words and Phrases
a bit of (something) - see Troublesome Words and Phrases
a few - see Troublesome Words and Phrases
a good (or great) deal of (something) - see Troublesome Words and Phrases
a handful of (something) - see Troublesome Words and Phrases
a large number of(something) - see Troublesome Words and Phrases
a little - see Troublesome Words and Phrases
abbreviations - see Troublesome Words and Phrases
ability to --- - see Troublesome Words and Phrases
abstract (common) nouns – nouns that are used for concepts, which have
  no material existence, e.g. $\Rightarrow$ anger. They describe ideas or qualities instead
  of something physical such as a house(it is a concrete thing).
absurd and ridiculous - see Troublesome Words and Phrases
abuse and misuse - see Troublesome Words and Phrases
academic - see Troublesome Words and Phrases
account (to or for something) - see Troublesome Words and Phrases
acquaint (-somebody/yourself with something) - see Troublesome Words
  and Phrases
acronyms - see Troublesome Words and Phrases
active verb – when the subject performs the action or experiences the state
  or condition, e.g. $\Rightarrow$ I write a letter.
active voice – same as active verb. Here is another example: she has won the
  first prize. She $\Rightarrow$ subject and performs the action of winning.
  See $\Rightarrow$ active verb.
acute - see Troublesome Words and Phrases
acumen - see Troublesome Words and Phrases

AD(from Latin 'Anno Domini') - see Troublesome Words and Phrases

ad hoc - see Troublesome Words and Phrases

adding relative clause – it is separated from the main clause by two
commas. It gives some additional information about the headword,

   e.g. ⇒ Frank, *who is Elina's friend*, is working abroad

       relative clause ↵

adjective – a word that modifies/qualifies the meaning of a noun, or

  pronoun, e.g. ⇒ she is **kind**.

adjective phrase – a phrase which has an adjective in it,

  e.g. ⇒ she is very beautiful. In this sentence: 'very beautiful' is an
adjective phrase and the headword 'beautiful' is an adjective.

adverb – the most common function of an adverb is to modify the main verb

  in a sentence, e.g. I can do it *easily*. easily ⇒ adverb.

adverb phrase – it can be an adverb on its own e.g. ⇒smoothly. It can also

  be part of a phrase, which has an adverb as its headword (see ⇒headword),

  e.g. very abruptly ⇒ very ⇒headword.

adverbial clause – in a complex sentence, it modifies the main clause, e.g. I
will talk to you when I meet you tomorrow. An adverbial clause is joined to

  the main clause by the conjunction ⇒ when.

adverbial element/ phrase – a part of a sentence which gives the least
compulsory information in a sentence : I wrote this letter in a great hurry.

                          adverbial element ↵

affect(and effect) - see Troublesome Words and Phrases

agent – in an active clause/sentence, the subject is doing the action. It is

  known as the agent, e.g. ⇒I write it. Here, agent ⇒ I. In a passive clause,
an agent comes after *by*, e.g. the letter is signed by *Anne*.

agnostic(and atheist) - see Troublesome Words and Phrases

agreement (or concord) – it is a rule in accordance with the verb form
which is agreed with the subject and number of the subject (singular/plural),

  e.g. ⇒ she sings. On the other hand, e.g. ⇒ they cry.

alibi - see Troublesome Words and Phrases

all ready (already) - see Troublesome Words and Phrases

all right - see Troublesome Words and Phrases

all together(and altogether) - see Troublesome Words and Phrases

already - see Troublesome Words and Phrases
allusion(to something/someone) - see Troublesome Words and Phrases
alternate(and alternative) - see Troublesome Words and Phrases
alternative - see Troublesome Words and Phrases
although - see Troublesome Words and Phrases
altogether - see Troublesome Words and Phrases
amiable(and amicable) - see Troublesome Words and Phrases
amicable - see Troublesome Words and Phrases
ampersand -& - see Troublesome Words and Phrases
annex/annexe - see Troublesome Words and Phrases
any - see Troublesome Words and Phrases
anybody - see Troublesome Words and Phrases
any longer - see Troublesome Words and Phrases
any more - see Troublesome Words and Phrases
anyone - see Troublesome Words and Phrases

apostrophe – a punctuation mark, e.g. ⟹ Joan's father is a phrase in which the apostrophe is placed between Joan and s to indicate the possessive case. For other usage, see punctuation.

apposition – when in a sentence or clause, two noun phrases come one after the other and both refer to the same thing, then phrases are in apposition,

e.g. ⟹ Mr Brown, our director, is retiring today.

apprehend(and comprehend) - see Troublesome Words and Phrases

article – there are two types of articles: **a** and **an** ⟹ indefinite article and

the ⟹ definite article.

as - see Troublesome Words and Phrases

asterisk '*' – it is a star symbol used as a punctuation mark to indicate the omission of letters, the importance of a particular word , a reference or a footnote at the bottom of the text, or elsewhere.

at - see Troublesome Words and Phrases
at this moment in time - see Troublesome Words and Phrases
atheist(and agnostic) - see Troublesome Words and Phrases
attributive adjective – it comes before a noun or clause, e.g.
my **new** car has arrived.
auxiliary verb – a small number of verbs such as **be**, **will**, **have** are used
with ordinary verbs, such as *work*. See modal auxiliary verb
awake(and wake) - see Troublesome Words and Phrases
awake to something - see Troublesome Words and Phrases

B

back up/backup - see Troublesome Words and Phrases
backward/backwards - see Troublesome Words and Phrases
bare infinitive – verbs without the particle *to* e.g. ⇒ talk . Bare infinitive is
   the base form.
barely(also hardly and scarcely) - see Troublesome Words and Phrases
base form ,(*root form* or *stem*) – verbs as listed in a dictionary, e.g. ⇒ walk
Before Christ(BC) - see Troublesome Words and Phrases
beside and besides - see Troublesome Words and Phrases
between (--- --- me/I) - see Troublesome Words and Phrases
bloc/block - see Troublesome Words and Phrases
bona fide - see Troublesome Words and Phrases
bottom out - see Troublesome Words and Phrases
bottom line(or the bottom line) - see Troublesome Words and Phrases
brackets – in British English, for writing purposes, the round brackets ( )
   which are known as parentheses are used. They indicate alternatives,
   include abbreviations or show additional information.
breakdown/ break down - see Troublesome Words and Phrases
breath/breathe - see Troublesome Words and Phrases
broach/brooch - see Troublesome Words and Phrases

C

calendar/calender - see Troublesome Words and Phrases
can(and may) - see Troublesome Words and Phrases
cannon/canon - see Troublesome Words and Phrases
cannot/ can not/can't - see Troublesome Words and Phrases
canvas/canvass - see Troublesome Words and Phrases
capacity for --- - see Troublesome Words and Phrases
cardinal numbers – a whole number, e.g. ⇒ 1,2,3.
censor/censure - see Troublesome Words and Phrases
chronic - see Troublesome Words and Phrases
circa(from Latin) - see Troublesome Words and Phrases
classifying relative clause – it describes the head noun in the main clause
   by its nature or type. It does not have commas around it, e.g. ⇒ she likes
   John *who is very intelligent.* John ⇒ head noun.
clause – it is a group of words containing a finite verb, and any other verb
   complement, e.g. ⇒ he went home early tonight.

clause elements – there are five clause elements: subject, verb, object, complement and adverbial. A clause may have some or all of these elements.

clause of manner – it tells us the way something is done or someone's behaviour, e.g. ⇒ I don't work **like he does**.

collaborate/cooperate - see Troublesome Words and Phrases

collective noun – a noun that refers to a group of objects, or things or people e.g. ⇒ team, committee, government.

colon ':' – a punctuation mark. It is used for different purposes.

comma ',' – like the full stop, it is a common punctuation mark. There is a tendency to use too many or too few commas. See ⇒punctuation

common noun – nouns that that refer to many of the same type of things, places, objects or people, e.g. country ⇒ there many countries in the world. People ⇒ there are millions of people in the world.

comparative clause – this is used to express comparison, e.g. Anne is less interested in eating out *than her husband*. It is introduced by the subordinators *than* or *as*. It is a subordinate clause.

comparative form of adjective – for comparing two things or people, e.g. ⇒ he is older than me. old ⇒ adjective and older ⇒ comparative form (oldest ⇒superlative form).

comparatively/relatively - see Troublesome Words and Phrases

complement – a noun or adjective phrase that follows a linking verb, e.g. ⇒ she is the *champion*. See ⇒ copula verb and **see** ⇒linking verb.

complex sentence – in a complex sentence, one clause is a main clause, with one or more subordinate clauses, e.g. ⇒ I telephoned my wife when I arrived at Heathrow Airport. Main clause ⇒ underlined.

compound sentence – a compound sentence has at least two clauses of equal status which are joined together with a coordinating conjunction, e.g. he lives downstairs and I live upstairs.

compound word – it is composed of two or more words, e.g. mother-in-law.

comprehend - see Troublesome Words and Phrases

concord - see ⇒ agreement.

concrete noun – a tangible thing that can be seen or touched is a concrete noun, e.g. ⇒ book. These are common nouns. see also ⇒ abstract noun.

conditional clause – it is constructed when you want to talk about a possible

situation and the likely outcome. It usually begins with if, e.g.
if she comes, she will try to take over.

confidant/confident - see Troublesome Words and Phrases

conform to/with - see Troublesome Words and Phrases

conjunction – a conjunction functions as either a coordinating or
subordinating conjunction, and joins clauses, e.g. ⇒ when in:
I will meet you *when* you are upstairs.

connection between/with - see Troublesome Words and Phrases

consensus - see Troublesome Words and Phrases

consequent/consequential - see Troublesome Words and Phrases

cooperate - see Troublesome Words and Phrases

coordination of phrases – it means joining together two phrases or clauses
of the same status.

coordinator – a coordinator is a coordinating conjunction, e.g. ⇒ and, but,
or. It joins clauses of the same status.

copular verb – it links the subject with a complement. The basic linking
verb is 'be'. There are only a few copular verbs. These include be, appear,
become, seem.

countable(count) noun – it has singular, and plural forms and can be
preceded by a determiner such as **a**, e.g. She has a **cat**.

D

dare - see Troublesome Words and Phrases

dash '-' – a punctuation mark. It is used for a variety of purposes.

data/datum - see Troublesome Words and Phrases

deadly/deathly - see Troublesome Words and Phrases

debatable(and questionable) - see Troublesome Words and Phrases

declarative (sentence/statement) – its order is:
subject ⇒ verb ⇒ verb complement (if any).

declarative structure – it means the structure of a declarative sentence or
statement.

defective - see Troublesome Words and Phrases

deficient – see Troublesome Words and Phrases

defining relative clause – see ⇒ identifying relative clause.

definite article – see ⇒ article.

degree (adverb of) – a word such as very, rather, somewhat, quite, pretty. It
shows the extent of quality, e.g. ⇒ she is very clever. Here, very ⇒ adverb
of degree.

demonstrative pronoun – it is used to refer to a particular person, or thing, e.g. ⇒ this is a car. Other demonstrative pronouns are that, these and those. These are also demonstrative determiners.

dependent clause – it cannot stand alone, e.g.

when I gave him a cup of tea, he drank it fast.

despatch/dispatch - see Troublesome Words and Phrases

despite - see Troublesome Words and Phrases

determiner - a simple word that is placed before a noun phrase, e.g. this.

direct object – I gave students passes. In this sentence: passes ⇒ direct object because the direct effect of the verb *gave* is on passes.

direct speech – the exact words of the speaker which are enclosed within the quotation marks, e.g. ⇒ ' We were aware of your financial problems,' said the chairman. It is quoted in someone's words.

dispatch - see despatch/dispatch

disinterested/uninterested - see Troublesome Words and Phrases

doubtful - see Troublesome Words and Phrases

dubious - see Troublesome Words and Phrases

dummy subject – when the word *it* or *there* is used in the subject position and does not relate to any specific thing, e.g. ⇒ It appears she is late again.

E

each - see Troublesome Words and Phrases

each other/one another - see Troublesome Words and Phrases

effect(and affect) - see Troublesome Words and Phrases

e.g. - see Troublesome Words and Phrases

either - see Troublesome Words and Phrases

either --- or--- - see Troublesome Words and Phrases

ellipsis – usually three dots are used to indicate that some words are left out, e.g. ⇒ get the---out of here!

embedded prepositional phrase – prepositional phrases are embedded in the noun phrase, e.g. ⇒ you spoke to Rachel about her journey. In this sentence: [Rachel about her journey] ⇒ noun phrase and [about her journey] ⇒ prepositional phrase.

empty subject – see ⇒ dummy subject.

et.al. - see Troublesome Words and Phrases

etc. - see Troublesome Words and Phrases

even though - see though

everybody - see Troublesome Words and Phrases

everyone - see Troublesome Words and Phrases

exclamation mark – it is a punctuation mark represented by ! e.g. Cheers! It is a terminator.

F

facetious - see Troublesome Words and Phrases

facility - see Troublesome Words and Phrases

factitious - see Troublesome Words and Phrases

farther/further/farthest/furthest - see Troublesome Words and Phrases

farthest - see farther/further/farthest/furthest

fatal - see Troublesome Words and Phrases

fateful - see Troublesome Words and Phrases

female - see Troublesome Words and Phrases

fictitious - see Troublesome Words and Phrases

finite clause – He walks to work. In this clause, the verb walk is marked for tense $\Rightarrow$ present tense. When in a clause the verb is marked for tense it is called a finite clause. See $\Rightarrow$ non-finite clause

finite phrase and finite verb – a finite verb or finite phrase such as *talk, went, was going, will be* are finite verbs and finite phrases. These are marked for tenses, e.g. $\Rightarrow$ he is singing a song. In this clause, the finite phrase is singing and is marked for tense $\Rightarrow$ present continuous.

footnote – it is a punctuation mark. It is written below the text to give further information.

forbear/forebear - see Troublesome Words and Phrases

former - see latter/former

fraction – a number which is not a whole number, e.g. $\Rightarrow$ half, two-thirds, four fifths.

full stop – it is the most commonly used punctuation mark. In the USA it is called a period.

furthest - see farther/further/farthest/furthest

future (simple tense) – it is a state or action that will take place in the future, e.g. $\Rightarrow$ I will come. It is: auxiliary verb(will/shall) + bare infinitive verb.

future continuous(progressive)– it expresses a state or action that will continue in the future. It is constructed as $\Rightarrow$ shall/will + participle –ing form, e.g.$\Rightarrow$ *I will be thinking of you.*

future perfect – it refers to our thinking in the future and then looking back when something will be completed at a specific point in the future,

e.g. ⇒ By next Friday, I will have met him in Paris. It is constructed as:
will/shall + have + past participle.

future perfect progressive – it is as future perfect, but the action. or state of something continues in the future, e.g. ⇒ Next month, you will have been studying at the university one year. It is constructed as:
will/shall + have been + participle –ing form.

G

gender/sex – in English the gender classification is: feminine ⇒ woman, masculine ⇒ man, and neuter ⇒ artefacts/things such as radio.
see also - see Troublesome Words and Phrases

gerund – When a participle verb formed with *-ing* is used in a clause or a sentence as a noun, it is known as a gerund, e.g. *Dancing* is her favourite hobby. In this sentence, dancing is a gerund.

glutton – see Troublesome Words and Phrases

gourmand - see Troublesome Words and Phrases

gourmet – see Troublesome Words and Phrases

grammar – it has rules for combining words together for a meaningful communication in spoken and written language.

gray/grey - see Troublesome Words and Phrases

gipsy/gypsy - see Troublesome Words and Phrases

H

half - see Troublesome Words and Phrases

hardly - see Troublesome Words and Phrases

headword – it is a main noun or pronoun in a phrase, clause or sentence. For instance: a **bundle** of files. a paperback **book**. Headwords are highlighted.

hopefully - see Troublesome Words and Phrases

however - see Troublesome Words and Phrases

hyphen '– ' – it is a punctuation mark. It is used either to join two words together or to split the word at the end of a line of print.

I - see Troublesome Words and Phrases

identifying (relative) clause – its purpose is to identify the earlier noun in the main clause, e.g.⇒ 'The young man **who is smartly dressed** is my son.'

idiom or idiomatic expression – it is a group of words. Its meaning is different from the meaning of individual words forming the idiomatic expression.

illusion - see Troublesome Words and Phrases

imperative(mood/sentence) – it is a command and an order. It can also be a polite order, e.g. ⇒ *forgive me.* **go away. please take a seat.** There is no subject and the verb is in the base form.

impracticable - see Troublesome Words and Phrases

impractical - see Troublesome Words and Phrases

indefinite article – see ⇒ article.

indefinite pronoun – a word which does not refer to any particular person or thing, e.g. ⇒all.

independent clause – see ⇒ main clause

indicative(mood/statement) – when we make a statement, ask a question or state a fact, e.g. ⇒ I'm here.

indirect object – see ⇒ direct object.

indirect speech – it is not in the words of the speaker but its meaning is reported in our own words, e.g. ⇒ I said she told me about her love affairs.

infinitive – it is the base form of the verb. e.g. ⇒ **go**. See ⇒ base form and bare infinitive (without the participle to-) as shown in dictionaries.

infinitive clause – it has an infinitive verb, e.g. We **walk** every evening. I wanted **to go**.   bare infinitive ↵

       to-infinitive ↵

inflection – it means changing the ending or spelling of a word in accordance with its grammatical function, e.g. ⇒ She studies French. The verb **'study'** is inflected to match the present tense of its subject.

informal English (style) – the use of the English language in social circumstances, e.g. both - spoken and written communication between relatives and friends.

ing- form – when *-ing* is added to a verb and used as a participle, or gerund e.g. write⇒writing.

interjections – a minor class of word. Used for expressing feelings,

e.g. ⇒ *Gosh!*

in spite of - see Troublesome Words and Phrases

interrogative pronoun – what and which are used with nouns to ask

questions, e.g. ⇒*Which* book was it?

intransitive verb – it does not take an object or complement, and it can stand

alone, e.g. ⇒ I talk.

inversion – it occurs when the regular word order is changed to form a

question, e.g. ⇒ Has she finished that job? In this sentence: the subject *she*

has changed (inverted) place with the auxiliary verb *has*.

irregular verbs– they do not follow the pattern of adding '-ed' to form the

past tense, e.g. ⇒ begin: its irregular past tense ⇒ began.

isn't - see Troublesome Words and Phrases

it's - see Troublesome Words and Phrases

its - see Troublesome Words and Phrases

inward- see Troublesome Words and Phrases

inward-looking - see Troublesome Words and Phrases

inwards - see Troublesome Words and Phrases

J

jargon - see Troublesome Words and Phrases

judicial - see Troublesome Words and Phrases

judicious - see Troublesome Words and Phrases

K

kind(kind of) - see Troublesome Words and Phrases

kindly - see Troublesome Words and Phrases

L

latter/former - see Troublesome Words and Phrases

leading question - see Troublesome Words and Phrases

legible/readable - see Troublesome Words and Phrases

lethal - see Troublesome Words and Phrases

licence - see Troublesome Words and Phrases

license - see Troublesome Words and Phrases

linking verb –see ⇒ copular verb. Linking and copular both mean the same.

M

main clause – any clause which can stand alone is a main clause, e.g. ⇒ I walk. It stands alone as a meaningful clause or a short sentence.

main verb – it is the finite verb in the main clause, e.g. ⇒ When the door bell rang, I *opened* the door.

majority - see Troublesome Words and Phrases

male - see Troublesome Words and Phrases

manner – it is the adverb of manner. It tells us *how* something happened, e.g. ⇒ she cried *loudly*.

mass noun – it is an uncountable noun. It refers to things such grass, hair, sugar, medicines. Sometimes it can be used as a countable noun, e.g. two sugars. one hair. It is used for quantities.

me - see Troublesome Words and Phrases

media(the) - see Troublesome Words and Phrases

minority - see Troublesome Words and Phrases

misuse - see Troublesome Words and Phrases

modal auxiliary verb – these are auxiliary verbs, e.g. ⇒ can, could, may, might, etc.

modify (modifier) – it means giving further information about a word or phrase, e.g. ⇒ It is a *tall* tree. 'tall' modifier is an adjective, but functioning as a modifier. It gives further information about ⇒**tree**.

myself - see Troublesome Words and Phrases

N

need - see Troublesome Words and Phrases

negative – a phrase, clause or sentence which has a word meaning 'no', 'not' is a negative phrase, clause or sentence. You can have a negative question as well. For instance: Didn't you shout at her?

negative word – a word like 'never', 'nothing' and 'nowhere' is a negative word, e.g. I can see nothing wrong with her idea.

neither - see Troublesome Words and Phrases

neither --- nor --- - see Troublesome Words and Phrases

nevertheless/nonetheless - see Troublesome Words and Phrases

nice - see Troublesome Words and Phrases

non-finite clause – it has a to-infinitive form verb, $\Rightarrow$ We asked them *to return* our camera.

none - see Troublesome Words and Phrases

none of something - see Troublesome Words and Phrases

nonetheless - see Troublesome Words and Phrases

nor/or - see Troublesome Words and Phrases

noun – it is a name given to a person, place, object, etc.,

e.g. $\Rightarrow$ John, London, book ….

noun (nominal) clause – it can act as the subject, object or the complement of the main clause, e.g. $\Rightarrow$ He thought *that she was not at home*. Here, the noun clause is acting as an object.

noun phrase – it has a noun or pronoun as its headword, e.g. $\Rightarrow$ I wanted John *as our leader*.

number – in grammar, the distinction between singular and plural is

expressed as number, e.g. cap $\Rightarrow$ singular noun and two caps(plural)

number of the same object $\Rightarrow$ cap.

O

object – it comes after the verb in a clause. For example:

this is Andrew. object $\Rightarrow$ Andrew.

object complement – it comes after the verb in a clause,

e.g.$\Rightarrow$ we all paid her **our** respects.

object predicate – see $\Rightarrow$ object complement.

one another - see Troublesome Words and Phrases

onward - see Troublesome Words and Phrases

onwards - see Troublesome Words and Phrases

oral/verbal - see Troublesome Words and Phrases

ordinal numeral – it refers to the position of something in a series, e.g. $\Rightarrow$ he was in *third* place. Some other examples: fourth, fifth, , hundredth, etc.

ordinary verb – there are thousands of ordinary verbs, such as $\Rightarrow$ go, run, jump, write, etc. Auxiliary verbs are not included in ordinary verbs.

over/under - see Troublesome Words and Phrases

P

participle – it is a non-finite verb form. It ends either with *–ing* or *-ed*.
See ⟹ present and past participle.

particle – it is the word *to* with the base form of the verb, e.g. ⟹ to run.

particles class – it is a minor word class, e.g. ⟹ she *fell off* her bicycle on to the road.

particular - see Troublesome Words and Phrases

passive – in a passive clause/sentence something is done to the subject

(agent), e.g. ⟹ the report *is being typed*.

passive verb (or passive voice) – when the subject is affected by the action. The passive voice involves the use of the **auxiliary verb.** For instance, the

house **is** occupied. Here is ⟹ auxiliary verb.

past continuous/progressive – it expresses what was happening at some

point in time in the past, e.g. ⟹ I *was working* in London.

past participle form – Regular verbs: it ends in **–ed**. Irregular verbs: it ends

in some other ways. e.g. ⟹eaten, drunk, etc. In the perfect it comes after 'have, e.g. I have *finished* it.

past perfect – it is formed with 'had' and a past participle e.g. ⟹ she *had received* my letter.

past perfect continuous/progressive – it is formed with 'had been' and an

active participle, e.g. ⟹ We *had been dancing* all night.

Here, *dancing* ⟹ active participle.

past simple – it is the past tense, e.g. ⟹ they *returned* home. It tells what happened or existed at a particular time (then) before the present time (now).

perfect – it expresses an action completed by the present, or a particular point in the past or future. It is constructed with 'have' with the past

participle of the main verb, e.g. ⟹ *I have left* (present perfect), *I had left* (past perfect), and *I will have left* (perfect future).

perquisite/prerequisite - see Troublesome Words and Phrases

person (singular and plural) – first person ⟹ **I, we.** Second person ⟹ **you.**

Third person ⟹ *he, she, it, they*.

personal pronoun – I, you, he, she, etc.

phrasal verb – it is a verb combined with an adverb or a preposition,

e.g. ⟹ fall off, break down, etc.

phrase – usually, it has some words, e.g. ⟹ a white elephant. It can be just one word e.g. ⟹ rubbish! There are five types of phrases: verb phrase, noun phrase, adjective phrase, adverb phrase, and prepositional phrase.

plural (noun) – it means more than one, e.g. ⟹ a song is the singular form but songs ⟹ the plural form of the noun.

possessive determiner – it is a possessive pronoun, when it replaces a noun, e.g. ⟹ this is *my* car.

possessive pronoun – mine, yours, ours, etc. This coat is mine. Possessive pronoun ⟹*mine*

postmodifier(postmodification) – it comes after the head noun in phrases, e.g.

       It is a nice **car** <u>fitted with audio equipment</u>.

             postmodification ↵⟹ head noun

practice - see Troublesome Words and Phrases

practise – see Troublesome Words and Phrases

predicate – in a clause, it is the verb element and any other elements that follow the verb, e.g. ⟹ England <u>is the largest part of the UK.</u> The underlined part is the predicate.

premodifier(premodification) – an adjective (sometimes an adverb) that comes before a head noun is a premodifier. There can be several premodifiers, e.g. ⟹a **tiny shining** star. star ⟹ head noun/head word.

preposition – a class of word, e.g. ⟹ over, since, for. Also more than one word, e.g. ⟹ instead of.

prepositional phrase – it is the preposition plus a noun or an adverb e.g. ⟹ in our school, over there.

prepositions of relationships – express a variety of relationships. Most common are time and place.

prerequisite - see Troublesome Words and Phrases

present continuous/progressive – it is the present tense that shows the action is continuous.

present participle form – it is the part of the verb which ends in –*ing*, e.g. ⟹ missing, crossing, etc.

present perfect – it indicates that the action or state was complete in the near past up to the present time, e.g. ⟹ The parcel has arrived.

present perfect progressive – an action or state in the past which continues up-to the present time, e.g. $\Rightarrow$ it has been raining. It is formed as: have/has + been + active participle.

present simple – it is the present tense, e.g. $\Rightarrow$ I work. It expresses a current action or state.

principle - see Troublesome Words and Phrases

pronoun – a word used instead of a noun or noun phrase, e.g. $\Rightarrow$ *You* are kind.

purposely - see Troublesome Words and Phrases

purposefully - see Troublesome Words and Phrases

Q

Qualifier (s) – postmodifier and premodifier are qualifiers. A qualifier can come before or after a head word, e.g. $\Rightarrow$ He has a corner shop near here. corner $\Rightarrow$ premodifier and near here $\Rightarrow$ postmodifier element.

qualify – see $\Rightarrow$ modify

question – it is a sentence for asking a question, e.g. $\Rightarrow$ What's wrong with you?

Question tag – a short question at the end of a statement, e.g. $\Rightarrow$ She loves him, doesn't she?

question word – these are what, when, where, who, whom, which, how, whose, why.

questionable - see Troublesome Words and Phrases

quite - see Troublesome Words and Phrases

R

readable – legible/readable

reciprocal pronoun – it is used to express mutual relationships, e.g. $\Rightarrow$ they love *each other*. There are only two reciprocal pronouns each other and one another.

reflexive pronoun – it refers to the subject, e.g. $\Rightarrow$ They can do it *themselves*. I do it *myself*.

regular verbs – they change their forms in the past by following a set pattern of *–ed ending*, e.g. $\Rightarrow$ verb 'help' its regular past tense form $\Rightarrow$ 'helped'.

relative adverb – where, when and why are used in relative clauses as relative adverbs, e.g. $\Rightarrow$ the house *where* I was born.

relative clause – it modifies a noun, e.g. $\Rightarrow$ the salesman *who talked too* *much*. It is modifying the noun salesman

relative pronoun – it links a subordinate clause to a main clause, e.g. ⇒ it is not me *who* hit first.

relatively - see Troublesome Words and Phrases

responsible - see Troublesome Words and Phrases

ridiculous - see Troublesome Words and Phrases

S

scarcely - see Troublesome Words and Phrases

sentence – a sentence is the largest syntactic unit which has at least one clause.

sex – see gender/sex

s-form of the verb – it is the inflected form of the bare infinitive. It is formed with either *s*, or *es* added, e.g. ⇒ he *runs.* Here *s* is added. She *cries*. Here, cry is inflected by *es*.

should - see Troublesome Words and Phrases

simple tense – it is without the auxiliary verb, e.g. ⇒ I go.

singular noun – it means one thing only, e.g. ⇒ noun 'man' refers to only one person/man.

so - see Troublesome Words and Phrases

sort - see Troublesome Words and Phrases

split infinitive – the placing of a word or words between the *to* and the *verb* creates a split infinitive.

standard English – a form of the English language that is nationally used. For instance, broadcasting services use standard English. Speakers of other languages learn standard English.

statement – it is a declarative sentence which gives information. It is not a question.

stationary - see Troublesome Words and Phrases

stationery - see Troublesome Words and Phrases

structure - for our purpose, it means the way some words are arranged in accordance with the rules of grammar, e.g. ⇒ I went there.

style - it is a distinct way of doing something, e.g. writing or speaking in the language context. There are many styles. For instance, various styles are imposed on the use of idiomatic expressions.

subject –in a sentence, it comes before the verb, e.g. ⇒ he writes a letter. he ⇒subject/agent.

---

subject complement – in a clause/sentence it comes after a linking verb.
e.g. ⇒she appears *calm*.

subject element – it precedes the verb in a clause. It is the agent of an active
clause, e.g. ⇒ I'm writing this text. Here, I'm ⇒ **subject** or subject
element. It is also the agent of this active clause.

subject position – it is the first element in a clause, e.g. ⇒ she loves you.
subject ⇒ begins the clause.

subject predicate – see ⇒ subject complement

subjective pronoun – *I, you* (both singular and plural) , *he, she, it, they*
and *we*. They occur in the subject position in a clause.

subordinate clause – it supports the main clause. See ⇒dependent clause

subordinator – in a complex sentence clauses are of unequal status. We use
a subordinator (**when** …) to join two clauses of unequal status.

subsequent - see Troublesome Words and Phrases

subsequently - see Troublesome Words and Phrases

superlative – the form of an adjective for comparing three or more things,
e.g. ⇒ highest, tallest (adjectives).

T

taboo style – use of swear words.
See⇒Asterisk under punctuation

tense – it is a form of the verb which indicates when the action of the verb
occurs, or the state affected by the verb, e.g.

   . I talk ⇒ present tense

   . she cried ⇒ past tense

   . We will dance tonight. ⇒ future tense

It indicates a particular period of time or a point in time.

than - see Troublesome Words and Phrases

that - see Troublesome Words and Phrases

though - see Troublesome Words and Phrases

till - see Troublesome Words and Phrases

to-infinitive – it is a verb form which is preceded by 'to', e.g. to run, to sign.

to-infinitive clause – see ⇒ infinitive clause.

together with - see Troublesome Words and Phrases

transitive verb – it cannot stand alone and it is followed by an object,
e.g. ⇒ she *rang* the **bell**.

U

uncountable noun – it has only one verb form. Some uncountable nouns are only plural such as jeans, e.g. ⇒ **a pair of jeans**. On the other hand, some uncountable nouns such as **space** are only singular, e.g. space. When an uncountable noun is the subject, the verb is singular,

e.g. ⇒ Some *money is* in Euro currency.

uninterested – see disinterested/uninterested

V

verb – doing, action/state word. It is the most important part of speech,

e.g. ⇒ she *loves* her children. Without the word *loves* which is a verb, the sentence will not make any sense.

verb element – it is the focal point of a clause, e.g. ⇒ she <u>has completed</u> her assignment. In this sentence, the underlined element is the verb.

verb phrase – it is an ordinary verb, e.g. ⇒ run, have gone, etc.

verbal - see Troublesome Words and Phrases

verbals – these are derived from verbs e.g. ⇒ it was a *horrifying* scene.

voice – see ⇒ active verb (voice) and passive verb (voice).

vocabulary – it consists of words, e.g. all words in the English language.

W

wake - see Troublesome Words and Phrases

wh-question – it is the question which begins with a question word or wh-word, e.g. ⇒what, where., etc. See⇒ wh-word

wh-word – there are nine such words: how, what, when, where, why, which, who, whom, whose.

which - see Troublesome Words and Phrases

word class– it is another name for parts of speech, e.g. noun, verb, etc.

would - see Troublesome Words and Phrases

XYZ

'yes/no' question – a question which can lead to a simple answer whether **'yes'** or **'no'**, e.g. Were you present in the class at that time?

Index